insight text guide

Robert Beardwood & Kate Macdonell

Dream Stuff

David Malouf

First published in 2001, reprinted with revisions in 2020.

Insight Publications Pty Ltd
3/350 Charman Road
Cheltenham VIC 3192
Australia
Tel: +61 3 8571 4950
Fax: +61 3 8571 0257
Email: books@insightpublications.com.au

www.insightpublications.com.au

A catalogue record for this book is available from the National Library of Australia

David Malouf's *Dream Stuff* / Robert Beardwood & Kate Macdonell

ISBNs:
9781875882700 (print)
9781922378958 (digital)
9781922378965 (bundle: print + digital)

Cover design by Gisela Beer

Printed in Australia by Ligare

contents

CHARACTER TABLE

Story	Setting: time and place	Children/adolescents	Outsiders
'At Schindler's'	**Time:** during WWII. **Place:** Schindler's boarding house at Scarborough, on the Queensland coast.	Jack, son of Milly and Stan. The narrative adopts his point of view throughout.	Jack: he is told 'You talk like a Yank' (p.17).
'Closer'	**Time:** present day. **Place:** a country property in NSW.	Amy, nine, in a religious (Pentecostal) family, being educated by her grandmother.	Charles Morpeth, Amy's uncle, is banished by his parents because of his homosexuality.
'Dream Stuff'	**Time:** present day, with details of Colin Lattimer's past. **Places:** Brisbane; more briefly, Athens and London.	Colin, as he remembers himself as a child; Marcus, the son of Colin's partner, Emma, who is 'easy and serious and assured' (p.60).	Colin: 'He knew no one in Brisbane but his cousin Corrie' (p.38).
'Night Training'	**Time:** 1951, during the Korean War. **Place:** Training camp for soldiers of the University Air Squadron.	Greg Newsome and Cam Brierly, both seventeen: 'They stuck together ... to conceal from others their appalling innocence' (p.65).	Dave Kitchener is 'a bit of an outsider with his fellow officers' (p.66).
'Sally's Story'	**Time:** near the end of the Vietnam War (1957–75). **Places:** Sydney and a country town in NSW.	Sally Prentiss, nineteen, an aspiring actress who works as a war 'widow' to gain some 'real experience of life' (p.75).	Brad Jenkins 'lives out Duggan way' (p.84); a single father.
'Jacko's Reach'	**Time:** present day but reflects on the past of the unnamed narrator. **Place:** Jacko's Reach (formerly Jago's) near Sydney.	'Valmay Mitchell was thirteen' (p.97): her story shows how things could happen in Jacko's Reach that were outside social conventions.	People who spend time in Jacko's Reach: 'the derelicts who gather there ... the few local Aborigines who claim an affinity with the place' (p.93); Valmay Mitchell.
'Lone Pine'	**Time:** present day. **Places:** the bush, in northern Australia; places unnamed on the map; Hawthorn.	Kenny, the murderer, is a 'young fellow of maybe twenty' (p.107); Dale, 'ten or so' (p.106).	Harry and May have left behind their regular routines of work and home.
'Blacksoil Country'	**Time:** unspecified, probably mid-19th century. **Place:** frontier bushland, NSW or Queensland.	Jordan McGivern, twelve, narrates the story.	Jordan's father finds it difficult to find acceptance until Jordan is killed.
'Great Day'	**Time:** present day (late 20th century). **Place:** the Tylers' house, near Waruna, a small coastal town.	Ned, eleven, and Jenny, nine, are the children of Ralph and Angie.	Madge, Fran and Clem are outsiders in various ways, with respect to the Tyler family (to which they also belong).

INTRODUCTION

David Malouf was born in Brisbane in 1934 and is of Lebanese and English descent. During the 1960s and early 1970s Malouf published several collections of poetry, beginning with 'Interiors' in the anthology *Four Poets* in 1962. Malouf's poetry gained him increasing recognition in Australian literary circles, but it was the publication in 1975 of his first novel, *Johnno*, that established him as one of Australia's foremost writers of fiction.

The stories in *Dream Stuff* are set in Australia and take their general bearings from some pivotal moments in Australian history and aspects of Australian identity. In particular, Australia's twentieth-century wartime involvements provide the historical context for several of the stories. Typically, though, Malouf's interest is in characters whose lives are peripheral to the nation's main action.

The broad issues of settlement and attachments to place, including the colonial and contemporary relations between white and Aboriginal Australians, are touched on throughout *Dream Stuff*. The complex intersections and tensions between private (or personal) and public (or social) experience are always part of the way the stories explore historical and social issues.

The transforming power of dreams is a central theme in *Dream Stuff*. The apparent boundary between dreams and reality is often blurred; *Dream Stuff*'s exploration of dreams is intertwined with questions about the nature of reality and the nature of the experience of being human. At moments of extraordinary intensity, the experience of characters takes on dreamlike qualities. The complex relation between dream and memory is also explored, especially through the figure of the child and the experience of childhood.

Dreams and memories are also linked to the creative acts of writing and storytelling, giving several of the stories a self-reflexive quality. That is, they describe events and experiences in a naturalistic fashion, but they also explore the slippery, enigmatic qualities of language and narrative.

BACKGROUND & CONTEXT

Australian historical moments and settings

In *Dream Stuff*, several stories refer to significant aspects of Australia's history. These include the involvement of Australians in international conflicts during the twentieth century – in the stories 'At Schindler's', 'Night Training' and 'Sally's Story' – and, in 'Blacksoil Country', encounters with Aboriginal people on the colonial frontier. Other stories also allude to these issues, for instance in the title 'Lone Pine', and the wartime drowning of Colin Lattimer's father in 'Dream Stuff'. 'Great Day' has a contemporary setting, on a day of 'national celebrations', though the narrative does not explicitly name the historical occasion being celebrated.

National identity 'up in the air'

The historical events referred to in *Dream Stuff* are related to, and help to define, Australia's national identity. However, Malouf's interest is in incidents at a distance from the central action, in order to explore unusual perspectives on wartime or colonisation. *Dream Stuff* does not support the idea that Australia's history and identity are well defined. Rather, Malouf is more inclined to show how ambiguous and fraught identity is, especially national identity, than to establish its clear, absolute definitions and outlines.

The most well-defined image of national identity in *Dream Stuff* is that of the boy, Ned Tyler, in 'Great Day'. Ned envisages 'a bonfire on every beach and the whole map of Australia outlined with fire' (p.153). However, Ned's fervent nationalism is contrasted with the more reflective attitude of his elders, who 'never want anything settled' (p.152). The story, like the collection as a whole, suggests that identity and feelings of belonging to a group are never permanently settled. The tendency of Malouf's narratives, like the Tylers' own inclination, is to leave things 'up in the air' (p.152).

The world wars

Australia's involvements in the two world wars have been crucial to mainstream representations of Australia's history and national identity. The Dardanelles campaign of World War I (1914–1918) gave rise to the Gallipoli legend; this was the first time that Australian and New Zealand troops (the ANZACS) fought as independent forces, rather than being merged into the Allied troops. This legend is alluded to in *Dream Stuff* in the story 'Lone Pine' – Lone Pine was the location of one of the most famous battles at Gallipoli.

The war in the Pacific during World War II (1939–45) was the source of enduring stories about the resilience and heroism of Australian soldiers, many of whom became Japanese prisoners of war. Australia became the base for the Allied military operations in the Pacific, under the leadership of the US General Douglas MacArthur. As a result, many American servicemen were stationed in Australia during the early 1940s, and their superior pay, finer uniforms and more confident manner in comparison with Australian servicemen led to their having a significant social impact in Australian cities. This is the context for the opening story of *Dream Stuff*, 'At Schindler's': the narrative adopts the perspective of a Brisbane boy whose father is missing in action in the Pacific, and whose mother begins a relationship with a US serviceman.

The Korean and Vietnam Wars

As in World War II, Australia fought alongside the United States in subsequent international conflicts. The Korean (1950–53) and Vietnam (1957–75) Wars involved two Asian countries left internally divided (between north and south) after the end of World War II. The northern part of each country was under Communist rule (under the former USSR – the Union of Soviet Socialist Republics) while US forces were installed in the southern part. The United States was particularly concerned to stop the movement of Communist governments into South-East Asia and the Pacific region, and Australian governments supported the US position throughout most of this period. On the election of the

Whitlam Labor government in 1972, however, Australian troops were withdrawn from Vietnam.

The Korean conflict, in which Australian soldiers fought as part of a United Nations-sanctioned alliance of sixteen nations, forms a distant backdrop to the story 'Night Training'. In the Vietnam War, Australia was again an ally of the US and, as in World War II, United States servicemen were frequent visitors to Australian cities. One aspect of their presence is taken up in 'Sally's Story'.

Encounters with Aboriginal people

The violence of the colonial frontier throughout the nineteenth century has been a central issue in Australian history. In the last few decades there has been a radical shift in the way Australia collectively represents and argues over its past. The historical research and writings of Henry Reynolds, since *The Other Side of the Frontier* (1981), have argued compellingly that violence between whites and Aboriginals on the frontier was widespread and extremely destructive. Reynolds's work has consistently pointed not only to the systematic way in which Aboriginal people were hunted, killed and forced into submission, but also to the determined and frequently effective way in which Aboriginals fought back, strongly resisting the invasion and theft of their lands.

In the story 'Blacksoil Country', Malouf acknowledges that massacres – 'the unbridled savagery of slaughter' (p.130) – did occur on the frontier. However, his interest is not so much in the details (the historical facts and figures), as in the personal motivations and possible states of mind of those who set out on raids with the intention of killing as many Aboriginal people as possible.

Aboriginal people also play marginal roles in the stories 'Dream Stuff' and 'Great Day'. In both cases, their presence generates feelings of uneasiness in the white characters at the centre of the narratives, but Malouf does not take up an Aboriginal point of view in any sustained or focused way.

The role of dreams

Dreams play central roles in the first three stories in the collection; the other stories demonstrate more interest in experiences in which characters are fully conscious and awake, but which nevertheless have dreamlike qualities. These waking experiences include the invasion of Harry and May Pictons' caravan in 'Lone Pine', and Jordan McGivern witnessing his father shooting an Aboriginal man in 'Blacksoil Country'. What links the dream and the dreamlike experience in *Dream Stuff* is an air of unreality, due to the central character being placed in an unanticipated and confronting situation, and the suspension of conventional, everyday expectations and rules for behaviour.

The Viennese psychologist Sigmund Freud (1856–1939) developed the first scientific theory of dreams; his best-known work is *The Interpretation of Dreams* (1900). Freud sought to interpret his patients' dreams in order to understand their personalities and the underlying causes of their psychological disorders. Then, through analysis and discussion between the psychoanalyst and the patient, the condition could be treated – the 'talking cure'.

The return of the repressed

In Freud's theory, the unconscious is formed through the repression of bodily instincts, ideas and images, due to the individual's need to conform to social codes of behaviour. Although these acts of repression are a 'normal' part of socialisation, there are times when that which is repressed forces itself into conscious experience. Dreams, for Freud, are the most important instance of such a 'return of the repressed'; thus, 'the interpretation of dreams is the royal road to a knowledge of unconscious activities of the mind' (cited in Wright 1984, p.17).

Malouf's interest is not in the unconscious as such, but in occasions when impulses or insights that have been repressed – in order to fit in with attitudes that are sanctioned by one's family, or society – suddenly surface. This can be in a dream; for instance, in Amy's dream in 'Closer', her estranged Uncle Charles is miraculously reconciled to the family. Alternatively, that which has been repressed can surface in one's waking life, as when Jordan's father decides to express his hostility towards the local Aboriginals by shooting one of the men. Like Amy's dream, Jordan's experience of watching his father at this moment is one in which the normal rules of behaviour are suspended – indeed, his father's action radically transforms the rules of behaviour that apply in the rest of their lives, too.

Space and place

Alongside the historical issues and settings in *Dream Stuff* is an interest in the roles of space and place in individual experience, identity and relationships. Here we simply introduce a few concepts and terms, which are later taken up in more detail in the 'Themes, ideas & values' section.

The role of houses

In *Dream Stuff*, houses and other residences – such as tents, or the Pictons' caravan – reflect the lives and habits of their owners and inhabitants. Also, less straightforwardly, houses shape the lives and habits of their occupants. The tents of the holidaymakers in 'At Schindler's', for instance, facilitate an easy coming-and-going totally unlike Jack's orderly, well-regulated way of life in Brisbane.

In 'Great Day', the children sleep 'out on the deck' (p.184), reflecting – and reinforcing – that they are not significant within the family power structure. Marge, on the other hand, spends a lot of time in the kitchen, the centre of the house and the room around and through which other family characters congregate and flow.

Spaces in between: liminal zones

The stories 'At Schindler's' and 'Dream Stuff' are set in South East Queensland, where many houses share a particular architectural feature. Houses are raised well above the ground on poles or stumps, for cooling and to protect against floods. The space underneath the house is both 'outside' and also partly enclosed by the house. Such a space is an example of a *liminal* zone: a space that is contained and limited by what surrounds it, but that also, paradoxically, offers the possibility of an escape from the everyday regularities of space and time. This escape is double-edged: it is disorientating, but it also facilitates personal transformation and insight.

The space under the house, significant in Colin's dream of early childhood in 'At Schindler's', is perhaps the best example of a liminal space in *Dream Stuff*, but there are many others. They include verandahs (e.g. in 'At Schindler's'), beaches, various kinds of temporary, makeshift households, and property boundaries such as fences (in 'Closer').

GENRE, STRUCTURE & STYLE

The nine stories in *Dream Stuff* range in length from the very short (seven pages for 'Jacko's Reach', eight for 'Closer') to the very long (fifty-four pages for 'Great Day'). They employ a variety of Australian locations, identities and historical periods; individually, the stories stand alone in terms of their various characters and settings.

Connections between stories: imagery and theme

Dream Stuff's stories are linked in two related ways: through their common themes, and by their shared imagery. The most obvious connection between stories is the theme of dreaming, and the possibilities created by dreams for genuine transformation in people's lives.

Malouf uses imagery in a very economical, concentrated fashion. Images of water and various kinds of boundaries, especially fences, are deployed throughout, appearing either as objects within the stories or as metaphors for more abstract values and ideas.

Two types of story structure

The stories, with the exception of 'Great Day', are structured in two main ways. One of these structures applies to three stories: 'Closer', 'Night Training', and 'Jacko's Reach'. 'Closer' and 'Jacko's Reach' have a first-person narrator, while the third-person narrative voice of 'Night Training' is closely aligned with Greg Newsome. These stories are close studies of particular characters and/or locations, and have little or no plot. Indeed, 'Jacko's Reach' is more of an essay than a story, since the narrator reveals little about his own life experiences, and the story does not develop character or narrative tension in a conventional way.

In contrast, most of the other stories are structured around a key incident in the life of the central character. 'Lone Pine' and 'Blacksoil

Country' are shorter pieces in this group, both featuring a violent incursion into the main characters' lives. In 'At Schindler's', Jack's moment of insight occurs when he imagines seeing his father's ghost, but then recognises the mirror image as his own. Sally Prentiss's life changes when she returns home for a holiday in 'Sally's Story'; Colin Lattimer returns to the city of his childhood in 'Dream Stuff', only to spend an unsettling night in a Brisbane lock-up.

'Great Day' is different again. By far the longest story in the collection, it uses multiple narrative points of view rather than a central, organising perspective. There is no definite turning point in the narrative or in the characters' lives; its emphasis is on change occurring in cycles, rather than in violent, isolated moments.

Shifting narrative points of view

Although the stories are told predominantly from the point of view of either a first-person narrator (e.g. 'Closer') or a third-person limited narrative voice (e.g. 'At Schindler's', 'Sally's Story'), sometimes the narrative point of view shifts within stories. This reflects an understanding of reality as fluid – as not falling into neat, well-defined categories, but dependent on the narrative's perspective at any given moment.

For the account of colonial frontier violence in 'Blacksoil Country', the narrative voice shifts from first to third person, then returns to the first-person narrator who, by this point, is dead. Thus, even the categories of 'life' and 'death' are imaginatively merged into each other through the manipulation of narrative voice and point of view.

Malouf's prose style

Malouf's prose style is multi-layered and rich in meaning. Even the most common, ordinary object can be made symbolic in these stories, due to the way it is invested with meaning for particular characters, or described in terms of a metaphor or simile. A good example of such an object is the coffee table made by Rupe Tyler as a schoolboy, to which his brother Clem attaches a particular emotional, and almost spiritual, significance:

> He liked to run his fingertips along the edge of the coffee-table and feel the sand under its varnish ... Rupe's table had played no special part in his life till then, but he had clung to it, it had shored him up, and squatted now, an ugly, four-legged angel, right there in the centre of the room, very solid and low to the ground, bearing glasses and a lumpy dish full of cashews. He would have knelt down and stroked it ... ('Great Day', p.163)

The metaphor of the 'angel' invests the table with spiritual associations, but it is 'low to the ground', earthy rather than heavenly or elevated. Clem feels like kneeling – as if in prayer – and also like stroking the table, which adds a more sensual dimension not just to Clem but also to the table.

Complex sentences

Malouf's sentences are often long and ornate, with frequent insertions and clarifications. The middle sentence in the above quotation is a good example. Sentences often gain complexity by the insertion of clauses that indicate the narrative's perspective, or to emphasise that the statement being made is the opinion of a particular character, not of the narrator or Malouf himself.

An example of this kind of structural complexity in a sentence, again from 'Great Day', is the following: 'He was attracted, she saw, by her desperation' (p.165). The insertion of 'she saw' makes it clear that the narrative point of view is not omniscient, but limited. The sentence does not make an objectively true statement about a male character (Cedric Pohl) as the first three words suggest it will, but describes how that character is perceived by a woman (Fran) – and thereby also suggests how she perceives herself. This information, in turn, triggers a number of questions from the reader, such as: To what degree is what Fran 'sees' influenced by her own self-interest? Is she really all that 'desperate'?

The complex sentence structure employed by Malouf allows the stories to describe fine details and nuances of character while simultaneously opening up questions and uncertainties that are never resolved.

Imagery: a poetic approach to language

Malouf's prose is dense with images, not just in the description of settings but also in the development of character and incident. The rhythm and sound of a phrase or sentence are always important in Malouf's writing, which makes it very poetic. Consider, for instance, how the rhythms and sounds of the sea are present in this sentence from the opening of 'At Schindler's':

> The little waves of the bay, washing in and receding, dragging the shell-grit after them, would hush his body to their rhythm and carry him back to shallows where he was rolled in salt. (p.1)

Three short phrases, themselves like 'little waves', are balanced by the sentence's long final phrase – note how the use of commas generates and regulates this rhythm. The soothing sound of the ocean is mimicked by the selection of words containing 'sh': 'washing', 'shell', 'hush', 'shallows'.

Images that link the stories

Images of water play a significant role in *Dream Stuff*. Water imagery features especially in passages where the fluid qualities of objects and experiences are emphasised, as in dreams. The stories thus generate a sense of the interconnectedness of things and the slipperiness of seemingly secure points of reference. Related to this are the many references to ghosts and haunting throughout the collection. Past and present are thus figured as interpenetrating, with the past continuing to inhabit the present.

In contrast, images of walls, doorways, houses and fences gesture towards things that are fixed and can be known objectively; they suggest that experience depends on 'ground rules and the habits of a life lived on floorboards and in rooms' ('At Schindler's', p.22). The series of owners of the Tylers' house in 'Great Day' have 'added on in the style of the times' (p.132); the shapes of the house, and the lives of its inhabitants, have mutually determined each other over the years. There are different kinds of houses in *Dream Stuff*, not all of them as solid and permanent as the Tylers' – and sometimes it is their transitory, improvised nature that invests them with their possibilities for liberation, discovery, intimacy and dreams.

STORY-BY-STORY ANALYSIS

'At Schindler's' (pp.1–24)

Summary: *Jack's adolescence coincides with his father's disappearance in World War II. His mother, Milly, goes out with an American serviceman, Milt. They holiday at Schindler's in Scarborough. Jack sees his father, then realises it is his own reflection. Jack accepts that his father will not return and attains a new sense of wellbeing.*

In this first story, Malouf establishes a number of settings and themes that recur throughout *Dream Stuff*. The central character, Jack, is a child; the setting is the southeast Queensland coast; the nation is at war (in the Pacific); and finally, a dream and a dramatic, dreamlike experience combine to play a transformative role in Jack's life.

Jack's father

Jack yearns for his father, Stan, to return; he feels that his belief in his father's return is precisely what might bring him back, or at least keep him hanging on to 'whatever light thread was keeping him in the world' (p.3). Jack maps this connection in his head in the figure of a triangle, with Jack and Milly at 'two points' and 'the third point was over the horizon somewhere' (p.9). There are many competing triangles, due to the other relationships his mother forms. Milt, in particular, 'unsettled the map Jack carried in his head' (p.14).

Scarborough: the role of the coast

The sea and beach are present, both literally and as sources of imagery, throughout 'At Schindler's'. The tides transform 'what had just an hour ago been the bottom of the sea' (p.8) into a solid surface that connects Redcliffe and Deception.

The seaside town of Scarborough is a popular holiday place, bringing families to the camping ground in patterns that, over the course of the year, are tide-like: full at Christmas, empty during the winter. It is the place where Jack is 'most keenly aware of his body as the immediate image of himself' (p.9), yet Schindler's is also the place where Jack misrecognises his body's image in dramatic fashion.

Mirrors and the idea of the self

There are many images of mirrors and reflections in the story. As Jack stands on the diving board at Schindler's, the painted pool offers the 'ideal reflection' of the sky, and Jack reflects, in turn, on 'his father's stance up there' in previous summers (p.2). His father is 'missing', and the pool is empty – these two absences reflect each other, too.

When Milly realises Stan's 'missing' may be permanent, she contemplates a makeover with the encouragement of her sister-in-law, Susan. Jack, however, does not want things to change, especially his mother or her relationship with his father:

> The two figures in the mirror ... disturbed him; there was a kind of complicity between them ... He felt they had moved away into a place where he was not invited to follow. (p.4)

The mirror signifies the possibility of transformation, of discovering a new identity that is, in a way, no more than surface-deep. In another way it brings to the surface an interior, alternative identity, transporting the self into another place altogether. In contrast, the character who seems utterly unconcerned with appearances is Milt; his glasses are 'lenses without frames' (p.6), suggesting that Milt's view of the world is, despite the mediating influence of lenses, relatively free of limits or borders.

The most critical role of a mirror is during the storm, when Jack looks through the open French windows into his mother's room.

Key point

Jack dreams that he is on the slippery-slide platform, high above the beach 'with a king tide running ... water rushed and foamed out of sight below' (p.19). With its intimations of dramatic changes, violent flows of water and the confrontation of fears, the dream is a prelude to Jack's dreamlike walk along the verandah. In the dream, nature reflects as well as produces Jack's psychic state; the same holds true of the waking experience that ensues.

The verandah's exposure to the natural elements of the storm – 'rain was beating in under the rails, forming pools of lightning around every post' (p.20) – reflects Jack's return to a more elemental state, as well as his own openness to transformation. He imagines himself as 'a six-year-old still scared of the dark' (p.20), which is a form of release from present anxieties. The lovers too 'had freed themselves of all restraint' (p.20); this reminds Jack of 'moments when ... he ceased for a time to be a boy and became a porpoise' (pp.20–1). This form of imagined bodily transformation anticipates the real psychological shift Jack undergoes.

The 'ghostlike' image that Jack takes to be his father's, 'as if the world he belonged to was the otherworld of the dead' (p.21), is almost immediately recognised by Jack to be his own, 'fantastically elongated in the glass of the old-fashioned wardrobe' (p.21). Yet the mistake has a profound effect: it shows how desperately Jack has been projecting his desire for his father's presence onto his own being. When Jack sees himself *as* himself it is simultaneously a recognition of what Jack's insistence on the map inside his head is costing him – that the thread he imagines keeping his father in the world is really a thread holding *himself* back.

It is this thread that Jack hears, in the midst of the storm, 'snap' – with a sound 'louder than the crack of thunder' (p.21). Once it is broken, Jack becomes 'refreshed, restored', while also feeling a deep-seated loss, 'a shadow on his heart that would be there for many years to come' (p.24).

Q What is the significance of the swimming pool at Schindler's?

Q How does the Scarborough beach function as a metaphor – in other words, as well as establishing the coastal setting, what else does the beach represent?

'Closer' (pp.25–32)

Summary: *A nine-year-old girl, Amy, tells this story about her Pentecostal family. Amy's Uncle Charles has been banished from the family by her grandfather. Although it is never explicitly stated, it is clear that Charles' exile is due to his homosexuality. Amy dreams about, and longs for, Charles' return to the family.*

Although this is a simple story, told in the simple language of a child, 'Closer' is dense, fascinating and complex. As much is said by implication, in the gaps and silences of the narrative, as is said directly. The title hints at intimacy, but the content turns on separation and exile, and the painful nature of unexpressed thoughts and feelings.

Charles' sexuality, in terms of the words and ideas available to Amy, is unspeakable. Amy's silence on this question is a product both of her young age and the fundamentalism of the religion that dominates her thinking and her use of language. The fact that Charles is gay is conveyed most explicitly by Charles' phone call: 'This is GAY 437 calling' (p.27); it is confirmed by the reference to Sydney, where Charles lives, as 'Sodom'. Following his 'coming out' to his parents, Charles continued to visit the family's rural property at Christmas and Easter, but, in accordance with his father's wishes, without passing beyond the fence. However, at the most recent Easter, for the first time, Charles did not visit or phone his family. It is this absence that precipitates Amy's narrative and her dream.

'Dreams can be messages'

Amy's dream is a visual projection of her longing for Charles to return to the family. Charles' return is envisaged in fantastical terms: he walks straight through the fence, flowers spring up around his feet, and Amy experiences complete joy. This dream allows Malouf to articulate the significance of dreams not just for 'Closer', but for *Dream Stuff* as a whole:

> I knew it was a dream. But dreams can be messages. The feeling that comes with them is real, and if you hold on to it you can make the rest real (p.32).

The feeling that 'comes with' Amy's dream is the desire for Charles to come 'closer', for she and Charles to restore their intimacy.

The body and truth

Intimacy is represented in emotional and physical terms. Amy imagines that when she and Charles are reunited she will 'stretch out [her] hand and touch him' (p.32). Amy realises her grandmother's sense of loss is also felt physically, since she 'likes to touch' (p.29). In 'Closer', the body, and the closeness of bodies, represents a form of reality or truth. This truth is characterised by wholeness and by the existence of proof: 'he will be whole ... His laughter will be the proof' (p.32).

Writing and truth

Contrasting strongly with this version of bodily truth envisaged by Amy is the version of truth as that which is written in the Bible: the 'literal truth' (p.26). Since this truth is expressed in words, though, it can never be 'whole', and is entirely lacking in 'proof'. Instead of proof, it is Grandpa Morpeth's dominance that ultimately compels the family members to adhere to the written truths of the Bible. The three female members of the family – Amy, her mother (Helen) and Grandma Morpeth – all convey, in different ways, their disapproval of Charles' banishment. Adherence to the literal truth in 'Closer', then, results in exclusion and oppression, which is also associated with the power that the grandfather – the patriarch – wields in the family.

Despite Amy's assertions that 'all that is written in the Book is clear truth without error' (p.25), 'Closer' suggests that truths expressed in writing can *never* be 'without error'. Writing always contains gaps; the largest gap in Amy's narrative is the unspeakable nature of Charles' sexuality. One implication of 'Closer', then, is that inclusion and wholeness are sometimes only possible by moving beyond the restrictions and limitations of conventional, often patriarchal, social customs.

Q What is the significance of Amy's wish to become an astronaut?

Q Discuss the significance of the title, 'Closer'.

'Dream Stuff' (pp.33–63)

Summary: *Colin Lattimer, an author, returns to Brisbane following the death of his mother. He meets up with his cousin, Coralie. As Colin walks back to his hotel, a stranger attacks him and then tries to commit suicide. Colin is taken into custody and interrogated by police, then spends the night in a Brisbane lock-up. He is released in the morning.*

The title story is worth close attention, as it gathers together many images and themes that feature in the collection as a whole. These include the role of dreaming in life, and the dreamlike nature of intense experiences that dislocate people from their everyday worlds. The phrase 'dream stuff' is used explicitly in this story, referring to marijuana, though it could easily refer to several other things. The acts of dreaming, remembering and writing are closely intertwined in 'Dream Stuff'.

The author as character

Colin Lattimer resembles David Malouf in several ways. He is a novelist; he grows up in Brisbane and, as a young adult, moves to London; he bases his first novel on the Brisbane of his childhood. By drawing attention to the author-figure in the story as a reflection of the author in 'real' life, 'Dream Stuff' raises the interesting question of how the worlds of reality and fiction are intertwined.

Self-reflexive fiction

Colin imagines and manipulates characters as he writes in his Brisbane hotel, but later events produce in him an awareness that:

> some agency had taken over whose imagination was wilder than his own and which he could neither anticipate nor control. (p.49)

This introduces an interesting concept. Just as Colin creates his characters and their stories, so does Malouf. Colin is, of course, the product of Malouf's 'imagination'; the narrative is therefore *self-reflexive*

– it is writing that draws attention to itself *as* writing and to the process of writing. Rather than simply allowing us to become immersed in the story, Malouf makes us aware that he has created this story, that we are reading his fiction. This blurring of the boundaries between text and reality, of representation and the thing being represented, is a feature of postmodern fiction. Not all of these stories are postmodern in this sense, but 'Dream Stuff' in particular draws attention to the intertwining of text and reality at every opportunity. Even economics is likened to a story, with 'its own sort of drama ... the makings of a plot' (p.47).

Labyrinths and loops

Colin encounters a labyrinth when he follows in his father's footsteps in Athens, a city he 'had already wandered through in dreams' (p.39). His host leads him through a complex network of streets and lanes:

> They moved deeper and deeper into a maze ... everything here was a patchwork ... a tangle of narrow streets ... time was more a continual looping here than a straight line. He half expected, as a narrow street turned back upon itself, to see his father appear ... (p.40)

The maze, the patchwork, the tangle (or knot), the loop, and figures that turn back on themselves rather than moving on, occur repeatedly in Malouf's writing. They are metaphors for the nature of reality and life, which do not progress in an orderly, linear fashion but from point to point, with repetitions and odd turnings.

These figures also represent a model for an unconventional narrative that does not proceed in a straight line, in which expectations are not always met and tensions remain unresolved, but which ends at a point not very different from its beginning. This model certainly applies to Colin's life as it is represented in this story; and it also applies to the structure of 'Dream Stuff'.

Brisbane: present and past, surface and underneath

'Dream Stuff' has a strong sense of place, but after twenty-eight years Colin returns to a Brisbane that is considerably more urban than the one he left, so the visit constitutes a 'strange homecoming' (p.38). The former version of Brisbane may now be covered over, but in the imagery of the story it still has a presence, a kind of natural force which pushes up against 'flyovers, multi-level carparks, tower blocks … fathoms of poured concrete' (p.36).

Colin's childhood is also represented by a power which exists below the surface that continues to exert a force on, and in, the present. The story opens with two memories of childhood that are overlaid within Colin's dream. Colin had imagined that 'all that *underworld* of his early memories' (p.37, our emphasis) was accessible to him through his mother. Ironically, Colin's return to the place of his childhood is brought about by his mother's death.

Structure: two halves, like a mirror

'Dream Stuff' is in three marked sections, but really falls into two halves. The first half (parts I and II) provides background information about Colin's family and work. Part II focuses on Colin's long friendship with his cousin Coralie, which in the past has verged on flirtation and intimacy, but now is characterised by a greater emotional distance between them.

The second half, part III, contains the story's only real incident, which has a profound effect on Colin without significantly transforming his life. Colin is attacked by an unknown assailant as he walks back to his hotel; then the stranger attempts to commit suicide, and the police discover them grappling on the footpath. The real story behind his attack is never revealed, enhancing the dreamlike qualities of Colin's interrogation by the police and the night's remaining hours spent in a Brisbane lock-up. Although Colin is released the following morning he continues to feel, as if continuing to dream, 'in the dark' (p.58).

At one point in Part II, Malouf leaves the reader similarly 'in the dark' or suspended: the narrative indicates that Colin's marriage to Jane has ended, but gives no details or reasons for it. This is rather like Colin being left stranded in the backstreets of Athens, with 'the teasing suggestion of something more to come ... [in] suspended expectation' (p.41). To some extent these 'teasing suggestions' set the reader up for something to 'happen' in part III, though in the end the reader remains 'suspended' in 'Dream Stuff', rather than well satisfied.

The story ends with the same dream as it begins with, in which Colin is 'high up under the floorboards of the house' (p.63), nursing his mother's dying Doberman. The story is symmetrical, with the dreams producing a mirror effect. This contrasts with the traditional structure of a short story, in which the narrative tension gradually increases towards a sharp climax, then falls away in resolution. In 'Dream Stuff' there is no resolution and no progression to a new state of affairs. Moreover, Colin's 'earliest memory' of his childhood self is also a memory of death, which symbolically links, at the beginning and ending of the story, the beginning and the ending of life.

Q Discuss the significance of the many references to ghosts and haunting in 'Dream Stuff'.

Q Discuss the role played by images of plants in this story.

'Night Training' (pp.64–73)

Summary: *'Night Training' is told from the perspective of Greg Newsome, a seventeen-year-old cadet. It is 1951, at the start of the Korean War. Newsome and roommate Cam Brierly are the youngest members of the University Air Squadron's Intelligence Unit. Officer Dave Kitchener subjects them to sadistic night-time drills and lectures.*

This story explores the blurry boundary between dreaming and waking. Its central incidents are the 'night training' sessions experienced by Greg and Cam when Kitchener enters their hut 'somewhere between one and three in the morning' (p.73), makes them perform their drill naked, then lectures them on the realities of war. The enigmatic, seemingly pointless lectures reinforce the unreal, dreamlike qualities of these occasions.

In between waking and dreaming

Cam and Greg experience Kitchener's intrusions on their sleep and privacy in quite different ways. For Cam, sleep is 'like a membrane he was wrapped in that would not break' (p.68). This simile suggests that Cam is somewhat insulated from the 'night training' sessions. Kitchener says he wants to 'wake [them] up to things' (p.71); Cam, however, never seems to entirely wake up during these sessions. His 'membrane' of sleep suggests the membrane around a foetus in the womb, as if Cam remains so childlike he is yet to be born into the real world. The narrative repeatedly draws attention to Cam's childlikeness on these occasions: by his 'giggling like a child' (p.68); by Greg's manner of talking to him 'as to a three-year-old' (p.69); and by Greg seeing Cam's resolute sleepiness as a 'stubborn innocence' (p.70).

Greg wakes much more easily than Cam whenever Kitchener enters the hut, as if his own boundary between sleeping and waking is easily crossed. For Greg, the sessions are a 'dreamlike ritual' (p.70) with 'a quality of unreality' (p.73), but they are also intensely real. This sense of being in between two states of being, on an edge, is reinforced by the narrative's many references to edges and limits. Kitchener, for example, takes up a position not in the centre of the room but sitting 'on the edge of Greg's bunk' (p.68).

Rulers and rules

The central issue in Kitchener's lectures is of 'rules', which are clearly related to edges – this relation is made explicit by the use of 'a couple of ink-stained rulers' (p.69), in place of guns, in the night-time drills. These rulers also draw attention to the role of education in shaping and regulating the young men's lives.

In general, rules provide a form of limit or boundary within which it is safe to act. Outside these rules, however, people's actions and behaviour are less restricted. Kitchener's night-time intrusions transgress the rules of orderly camp life, and they are foreshadowed by Cam and Greg's early assessment that he 'couldn't be trusted to keep to the rules' (p.66). War, in the context of 'Night Training', provides the ultimate arena – one that is not actually entered in the story – in which the rules for human action might be radically altered, or entirely absent.

War as a noble endeavour

At the beginning of 'Night Training' the narrator describes Greg's conception of war. The phrase 'war seemed to him' (p.64) is crucial, since it means that all of the following statements about war describe *Greg's* attitude, rather than the attitudes of the story's narrator, or of Malouf.

Greg's understanding of war derives from a traditional, formal education (as indicated by the references to Plato), as well as his childhood memories of World War II. He sees war as able to harness what are normally opposing forces: primitive, animal energies and elevated, noble aspirations. In this view, war strips the individual back to the essential self, in the pursuit of a higher goal. This goal is the success of a larger, collective entity such as society, or 'the line of history' (p.64). The individual thus becomes a unified whole rather than a collection of contradictory impulses and fragments, whereby 'mind and body ... were instantly reconciled' (p.64).

The mind 'stays away'

Reading Plato provides Greg with a means of escape from the humiliating environment of his medical examination. He is made to sit naked, but he 'hung on mentally to his Plato' (p.65). Thus, 'mind and body' are not 'reconciled', to use the terms of the opening paragraph, but split. Interestingly, this split (or dualism) is also an important theme in many of Plato's writings.

War: 'another nature'

Greg's training does not alter this split between mind and body, as he imagines it will. In the passing-out parade, Greg experiences a 'kind of emptiness in himself'; his body obeys automatically but part of him 'had moved away' (p.72). The story ends with Greg's attitude towards military service being the opposite of his initial preconception of war as 'a natural thing' (p.64). Greg perceives that his body now belongs to 'another nature' (p.72), in which his movements follow a perfect, unthinking discipline.

Key point

This is the effect of 'training', both of the regular daytime routines and Kitchener's improvised night-time lectures: it is a training of the body to act entirely unnaturally. Far from mind and body being 'instantly reconciled' and in 'vivid exultation' (p.64), Greg's training for war leaves mind and body more divergent than ever.

Q What does Kitchener mean by 'The real war. The one that's going on all the time' (p.71)?

Q What possible interpretation(s) can you make of Greg's dream, described at the end of the story, in which he says 'No!'?

'Sally's Story' (pp.74–92)

Summary: *Sally Prentiss, nineteen, lives in Sydney near the end of the Vietnam War, as a 'widow' – she lives and sleeps with soldiers on their periods of leave. For a holiday, she returns to her mother's home in a country town. She meets, and spends the night with, Brad Jenkins.*

The role of the war

As in the other stories with wartime settings – such as 'At Schindler's' and 'Night Training' – the war plays a background role in 'Sally's Story'. The setting is Sydney during the Vietnam War (in the early 1970s) and Sally's clients are American soldiers. The war manifests itself through the men's nightmares and in the brief, artificial relationships Sally forms with them. The narrative describes nothing of the battles, or Australia's involvement, or even local protests against the Vietnam conflict. Instead, the focus is on individuals at the periphery of the action, whose personal lives are in some ways profoundly transformed by the war.

Structure and narrative point of view

'Sally's Story' falls neatly into two halves. In the first half, Sally lives in Sydney, occupying temporary homes, and involved in short-term sexual relationships that she enters in the name of gaining 'experience' for her future career as an actor. Note the significance of the name 'Prentiss': Sally is, at this time, like an 'apprentice', acquiring experience and skills for a profession.

The narrative voice is third-person limited; that is, the reader views the characters and incidents from Sally's point of view. Occasionally, though, the narrative adopts a more detached perspective, to establish setting and context. Such a perspective also allows the narrative slightly more knowledge than Sally has (of) herself – as in the phrase, 'she did not see, or not immediately' (p.91).

In the second half, Sally's reasons for acting in certain ways, and the feelings accompanying those actions, are the mirror images of those in the first part. She returns to a far more permanent home, her mother's, where Sally's younger brother and sister also live. This leads Sally to reflect on her past rather than anticipate her future: 'by the second day she remembered again why she had left' (p.81). She enters, almost by chance, a tentative sexual relationship with Brad Jenkins.

Sally and Brad

Sally's relationship with Brad has nothing to do with making money or acting a part for somebody else. Brad is a kind of widower, as his wife has left him – mirroring Sally's status as a 'widow' in the first half of the story. As a young, single father, Brad is something of an outsider with respect to the town. Yet, Sally discovers more comfort and human warmth in Brad's makeshift home than anywhere else.

The narrative indicates in several ways that Sally's intimacy with Brad is far more meaningful and real than her intimacies with American soldiers. The presence of Brad's children is an important factor: Brad performs a caring and nurturing role of which the soldiers had seemed completely incapable. This leads the narrative towards a consideration of intimacy between people in terms of what is essential and vital, as opposed to intimacy as a form of diversion, or even employment.

Breath

Images of breath play a significant role in 'Sally Story'. Breath comes from within a person, and is inextricably associated not just with life but also with speech and storytelling. Malouf employs breath to suggest things that are more profound, essential and real, especially in relation to identity. The soldiers, when they are dreaming of their wartime experiences, are seen by Sally to be 'gasping at the limit of their breath' (p.78); they are more comfortable, and more themselves, when telling 'some breathy story' (p.79).

In the case of Brad, and especially the baby, there is no such limit to breath. What Sally notices about Brad is 'the depth of his breathing' (p.91). This signals that Sally's perceptions of Brad are true, that they penetrate to his real, interior self. This, in turn, validates Sally's feelings of trust and wellbeing, even while in bed with an 'almost stranger' (p.91).

These feelings transform into a sense of liberation when Brad brings the baby into bed: then, Sally 'snuggled down and let herself float free on the unloaded breath' (p.92). These are the last words of the story. Although they are somewhat cryptic, they gesture towards a sense of self that is not acted or merely a 'breathy story'. Such a self that can be carried on the 'unloaded breath' comes from within, and can be discovered through the experience, however unlooked-for, of genuine care and intimacy between people.

Q Compare and contrast the domestic spaces represented in 'Sally's Story': the Sydney apartments, Sally's mother's house and Brad's house. What objects decorate and construct these interiors? Are these objects symbolic of more abstract values?

Q Discuss the images of nature, especially of weather, in 'Sally's Story'. How do these reflect Sally's circumstances and feelings?

'Jacko's Reach' (pp.93–100)

Summary: *An area of uncleared land, 'Jacko's Reach', is to be developed. The narrator reflects on past events in Jacko's Reach. Although he mourns the loss of such a space, he suggests that it will continue to exist in the mind.*

'Jacko's Reach' takes the form of a personal reflection, more like an essay than a conventional short story. The narrator sketches the history of the land known as Jacko's Reach, though without precisely locating it either geographically (in terms of known places) or historically. The story's present seems to be in the late twentieth century; expressions such as 'a skateboard ramp' and 'a Heritage Walk laid out with native hybrids' (p.93) help give the proposed development a familiar, contemporary resonance.

The lack of specific details about location enables Jacko's Reach to stand for any similar space, allowing readers to relate it to an actual place in their own experience. Local, official forces would regard such a place as undeveloped and unproductive – lacking in value – yet local individuals would place a high value on it. This tension is explored in 'Jacko's Reach', though without being completely resolved.

How 'Jacko's Reach' connects with the other stories

The narrative tends to generalise from the incidents described, so that their larger meanings and symbolism become evident. The story thus meditates on many of the ideas that are caught up in more dramatic contexts in the other stories. For instance, the idea of a marginal, wild space is also present in 'Dream Stuff', 'Lone Pine' and 'Blacksoil Country'; things being lost, the mourning of them and their persistence in the memory are central to 'At Schindler's' and 'Great Day'. 'Ghosts' are crucial to the patterns of imagery and metaphor in 'Jacko's Reach', as they are in 'Dream Stuff' and 'Blacksoil Country'. Intimacy is an important theme that helps to link 'Jacko's Reach' with the story immediately preceding it, 'Sally's Story'.

'Acceptable' human relations

In the past, according to the narrator, people related to one another through an 'older fellowship', which included 'gangs' and 'scratch teams' (p.98). These informal collectives are associated with a 'ghostly, dreamy area of ourselves' (p.98). In the narrative's present, however, dreams and ghosts are being suppressed. Allegiances between people are now formalised in such organisations as 'Rotary, or the Lions, or the BMA … the more acceptable ones' (pp.98–9).

The narrator's attitude towards these 'more acceptable' associations of people is a sceptical one; 'acceptable' here is ironic in tone. The narrator's sympathies are made clear by the fond recollections of the past's 'passionate loyalties' and the 'oddly moving' gatherings in the present of those who share the 'deeper affinities' and the 'freer and more democratic spirit' forged in the past (pp.98–9).

'Something so intimate': private versus public

One of the aspects of human experience made possible by a space such as Jacko's Reach is intimacy. The scepticism expressed towards 'acceptable' organisations may be understood in terms of a tension between private and public that centres their relation to intimacy. Jacko's Reach, for the narrator, represents a 'code-word for something so intimate it can never be revealed' (p.99). That is, it speaks for the private remaining secret and personal, rather than being 'revealed' and made public and 'acceptable' – at the cost of a loss of intimacy.

Structure: from nostalgia to defiance

There is no real plot in 'Jacko's Reach', but there is a noticeable shift in tone towards the end of the story, which gives the story a degree of structure and closure. The prevailing tone is reflective and mournful: the narrative represents the proposed development in terms of loss, rather than gain or profit. Unlike the other stories in *Dream Stuff*, 'Jacko's Reach' is strongly nostalgic, seeming to place more value on the past than on the present.

A shift to a much more defiant tone takes place when there are three short paragraphs in succession:

> So it will be gone and it won't be. Like everything else.
>
> Under.
>
> Where its darkness will never quite be dispelled, however many mushroom-lights they install in the parking lot. (p.99)

In contrast to the story's certain opening – 'So it is settled' (p.93) – these sentences suggest that the land will *never* be completely settled. They contain contradictions and paradoxes, implying that there is an inherent tension in the idea of progress. That is, progress, at least in the guise of the development proposed for Jacko's Reach, attempts the impossible: to put ghosts permanently to rest, to replace dreams with continuous lighting and 'solid, poured-concrete ramps' (p.99).

Ghosts and dreams, according to the narrator, will persist, since progress can only cover over, but not actually erase, the past. The tension in the idea of progress thus lies partly in the discrepancy between surface appearances and underlying realities. The *real* truth of the development of Jacko's Reach, the narrator suggests, is that its past histories and allegiances will live on despite the new polished surfaces; its past will be remembered and dreamt.

Q Describe the attributes of the narrator: what age, gender, sexuality, race and nationality do you ascribe to this narrator? Why does s/he not identify her/himself?

Q What is the meaning of the expression: 'will enter at last into … the dimension of the symbolic'?

Q What is the effect of the narrator comparing people and events to ghosts? Consider, for instance, references such as 'acts of violence … haunt the streets like ghosts' (p.97) and Jimmy Dickens 'continued to look out, in a ghostly way' (p.95).

'Lone Pine' (pp.101–15)

Summary: *Harry and May Picton are on a driving holiday. One night a young man, armed, invades their caravan, followed by a woman, a young boy and a baby. After a short confrontation, the man forces Harry and May to walk into the surrounding bush, then shoots them.*

Narrative tension and suspense

Malouf develops suspense in this story to a greater extent than in any other story. There is a strong sense of plot and controlled tension. Even the very first sentence strikes a note of unease: 'Harry Picton could have given no good reason for stopping where he did' (p.101). Once this note of uncertainty is struck, the narrative moves away from it, smoothly describing Harry's 'dreamlike' sense of driving through the country, then detailing the recent past of Harry and May in suburban Melbourne. However, the occasional, innocent-seeming expression (such as 'no need to worry. There were no predators out here', p.104), further heightens the reader's anticipation and unease.

The Battle of Lone Pine

Although this story does not have a wartime setting, the title alludes to a famous battle at Gallipoli during World War I. The capture of Lone Pine marked one of the furthest advances, and most hard-fought victories, of the Anzac forces during the Dardanelles campaign (April–December 1915). In Malouf's story, there is also a sense of foreign territory being occupied, if only temporarily, and a sense – as the story proceeds – of being under attack.

Personal battles

The 'battle' at Harry's 'Lone Pine' takes place when Kenny takes possession of the Pictons' caravan by force. However, the 'battles' that take place here are more personal and internal than physical and external, despite the violent end to the story. As we have seen, a sense of battles being fought internally, within the self rather than with an antagonist or opponent, is also hinted at in a more explicitly military context in 'Night Training'. Dave Kitchener lectures Cam and Greg about the 'real war', meaning not the events occurring in Korea but 'the one that's going on all the time ... now, in this room' (p.71).

Thus, in 'Lone Pine', Harry's desire to express to May 'all he wanted her to know and understand' (p.113) is never fulfilled, so that Harry's 'real war' is as much with self-expression, or with love, as it is with the intruders. It is almost a battle with language, which Harry has tended to forsake, preferring the solitude and comfort of his garden and to 'feel in his hands the special crumbliness and moisture of the soil' (p.106). This is an intimate solitude, a sensual connection between the body and the earth, but it is achieved at the cost of his intimacy with May. When she dies, Harry is left permanently without words: with a 'dumb, inconsolable grief' (p.114).

Even Kenny's desire to dispossess the Pictons of their car and van, and their lives, generates a battle within himself rather than with the couple. He walks them quite a distance from the van, a distance that 'had to do with his reluctance to get to the point, and was in himself' (p.113). Once he does 'get to the point', the narrative proceeds quickly, which heightens the shock of Harry and May's deaths after a relatively slow but steady development of tension.

Narrative voice

'Lone Pine' is narrated in the third person, mostly from Harry's point of view. From time to time, though, the point of view shifts to one of the other characters. For instance, May's perspective is adopted for much of the scene inside the caravan. This allows the narrative to convey her feelings about the magazine – she 'understood the youth's outrage because she shared it' (p.110) – and to end the period of dialogue and exchange with her realisation that 'it made no difference that he was calm' (p.112). Her apparent acceptance of what is about to happen shifts the tone dramatically from hostility and resentment to acquiescence and, especially for Harry, a profound sense of loss.

There are moments when the narrative becomes omniscient: the point of view does not belong to any one character, but to an external observer. An example is:

> Moving back and forth in the space between the bunks, [the woman] was rocking the child and sweet-talking it in the wordless, universal dialect ... that women fall into on such occasions and which sets them impressively apart. The others were hushed. (p.110)

This general, philosophical comment on women is quite distinct from the more prosaic language that characterises Harry's perspective and tone of voice, as in: 'she was a good woman spoiled' (p.105). The subtle shifts in narrative perspective add to the drama and tension within the caravan, almost like rapid changes in camera angles and perspectives in a film thriller.

Kenny's perspective and transformation

Kenny's perspective is adopted only after the shootings; no hint is given of his motivations or an explanation for the apparent lack of sympathy shown by Kenny and Lou for Harry and May. However, Kenny is transformed by his own violent actions, and it is his new state of being that the narrative is concerned with. His weight is the chief characteristic that alters: Kenny is now 'too heavy to move'; his real difficulty is to move on into 'whatever was to come' (p.115). This is, in a sense, the opposite of a dream happening, in which things proceed of their own volition, or someone else's. In Kenny's case, he must summon all his willpower to initiate the future. The violence at Lone Pine is now in the past, but it is not readily left behind.

The narrative thus makes a complete movement from start to finish, in terms of a progression from lightness to weight. The story's opening images are of clouds and water, evoking a sense of freedom and floating. The closing images are the opposite: Kenny looks up at the stars (recalling Harry looking up at the clouds overhead) but their light falls 'weakly upon him'. He feels like 'a swarming column', as if pressing into the earth and held to it 'by force of gravity' (p.115). When he walks away there is little sense of release, and the image of his family as 'dark and close' suggests, despite their newly obtained home and vehicle, an ongoing sense of weight and entrapment.

Q How do you think the pornographic magazine has come to be in the Pictons' van? What role does it play in the story?

Q What do you think Harry means by his 'inadequacies', and his 'demands whose crudeness, he knew, had never been acceptable to [May]' (pp.113–14)?

'Blacksoil Country' (pp.116–30)

Summary: *Jordan McGivern, twelve years of age, narrates this story. His family manages a farm on Australia's colonial frontier. His father shoots an Aboriginal man, then Jordan himself is killed in revenge.*

Comparison between 'Blacksoil Country' and 'Closer'

This story is similar to 'Closer' in a number of ways, which gives the collection overall a degree of symmetry, since 'Blacksoil Country' is the second-last story while 'Closer' is the second. The first-person narrators are close in age, and they represent a similar form of innocence. Each realises that a male at the head of their family – Amy's grandfather, Jordan's father – has acted inappropriately, and while they can appreciate the factors determining the actions of these men, they can also imagine alternative courses of action. That is, Amy and Jordan speak for a mode of behaviour that is more understanding and forgiving, one that desires intimacy and flexibility rather than power and the rigid enforcement of rules. Thus these two child narrators speak directly for many of the virtues of the child throughout *Dream Stuff* as a whole.

The dramatic contrast between 'Closer' and 'Blacksoil' lies in the conclusion of the two stories. In 'Closer', Amy's dream of reconciliation with her Uncle Charles leaves the story unresolved, with an air of uncertainty about what might happen next. In 'Blacksoil Country', Jordan is denied the chance to dream or imagine an alternative future, since he is killed. There is no possibility of reconciliation between opposing forces – between the white settlers and the Aboriginal tribes on the colonial frontier – within the frame of the story, since Jordan's father precipitates a massacre.

Boundaries and gender

Like Grandpa Morpeth, Jordan's father insists on property borders being respected; boundaries thereby become markers of exclusion and prohibition, policed by an adult (white) male. When Jordan says that blacks strayed across their (the McGiverns') 'rightful boundaries' (p.122), he reflects his father's, rather than his mother's, attitude to property. It is the father who would 'go out with a gun and shout at them' (p.123). His ability to police the boundaries gives him a form of power that otherwise has been mostly lacking in his life – the 'power to hold us in one place and safe' (p.119).

Jordan's mother, in contrast, adapts to the family's perpetual restlessness by establishing connections between one place and the next. These connections are made through the possession of personal 'bits and pieces' (p.118) and through *making* things: 'whatever strung the different places together was in what she made' (p.119).

Key point

The mother's work produces continuity and coherence while the father strives to shore up boundaries, making each place separate from another. What makes this male attitude to property unstable is that boundaries are not recognised in a universal fashion, largely because they are not part of the world of nature.

Appreciation of the natural world

Jordan understands the fundamentally arbitrary qualities of boundaries largely because he is so appreciative of the natural world. This is what generates his love for the 'blacksoil country', rendered in explicitly sensual terms: 'your kneecaps touching it ... you could see it, and smell the richness of it too ... I liked the voices of it' (p.122). The natural world is characterised in terms of excess and plenitude: it has 'richness' and is 'more than it looked', and when it floods the country is 'like a river as wide as the horizon' (p.120).

Jordan's delight in the abundance of nature is in stark contrast to the mean-spiritedness of his father, who 'screwed his eyes up against the glare of green'; and for Jordan's mother the country represents a 'kind of horror' (p.121). At the end, when Jordan is buried, he imagines its 'black' soil blending with his 'white grains' (p.130). This physical interconnection of black and white also seems to make new attitudes towards the land possible for his parents. The final image is of the mother 'raising her eyes to the land and gazing off into the brimming heart of it' (p.130); the family makes a connection with the land through, and despite, the loss of the son.

Shifts in the narrative point of view

'Blacksoil Country' is an example of Malouf's subtle shifts in narrative voices and tenses in what is, on the surface, an extremely simple story. The narrative voice is more complex than in the two other shortest stories, 'Closer' and 'Jacko's Reach', despite the simplicity of the language used (in keeping with the language of an uneducated, twelve-year-old boy). The tense shifts between present – 'This *is* Blacksoil country' (p.116) – and past – 'It *was* Blacksoil country' (p.120, our italics) – several times within the story's fifteen pages. The narrative voice also shifts into third-person for most of the final two pages, when it becomes clear that the narrator has in fact died, but returns to first-person for the concluding three paragraphs.

Key point

The implication of these narrative shifts is twofold: they blur the distinction between past and present, and they suggest that the moral considerations of events in the past depend critically on the historical narrative's point of view.

The emphasis of Jordan's narrative is less on judging the morality of his father's actions – Jordan unambiguously admits that his Pa 'was wrong every way' (p.126) – as on attempting to understand the feelings and motivations behind those actions. Thus, 'Blacksoil Country' has implications for how white Australia reflects on its past and comes to a degree of understanding and acceptance of the violence of settlement.

This understanding might be achieved not by insisting that the colonial frontier was not violent, but by *imagining* its context, imagining the fears and desires bound up with settlement, and acknowledging how white bodies and the Australian landscape have been intimately connected – in some ways as a direct result of violence – for more than 200 years.

Q Discuss the significance of the references to ghosts in this story. Are they ghosts of Aboriginal people, or white people, or both? Does it matter to which race a ghost belongs?

Q Discuss the ways in which 'Blacksoil Country' represents Aboriginal attitudes to land, boundaries, exchange and justice as being more 'natural' than white attitudes.

Q Consider how the meaning of Jordan's introductory remarks ('I am twelve years old. I can show you this country. I been in it long enough', p.116) is transformed by the events described at the end of the story.

'Great Day' (pp.131–85)

Summary: *The Tyler family celebrates Audley's birthday with a party; the story follows several family members over the course of the day.*

'Great Day' is fifty-four pages long, the longest story in the collection. This extra length allows 'Great Day' to acquire some of the complexities of a novel. Many of these complexities are taken up in the 'Characters & relationships' and 'Themes, ideas & values' sections, where their links to the other stories are also considered.

In keeping with the traditional form and scope of a short story, the range of times and places in 'Great Day' remains limited – the action takes place in the course of one day, and is mostly contained within a single house. There is no single dominant voice or perspective in this story; several characters are developed and given complex psychologies, histories and relationships within the family, providing the narrative with multiple points of view and rich dramatic interest.

Turning points and the 'great day'

The 'great day' of the title is Audley Tyler's seventy-second birthday, for which a party is being held at the Tylers' seaside house. The birthday coincides with a larger, seemingly national celebration that is never specified; the implication is that it is Australia Day, perhaps even in the Bicentennial year (1988).

The family as a whole downplays the national occasion, though this is mostly due to the men's attitudes towards it. Audley's son, Ralph, thinks they should be 'non-participants in the national celebrations ... "it's just a day like any other"' (p.152). The reader knows, through the perspective of Ned, Ralph's son, that this is Audley's opinion too.

Audley's wife Madge, however, declares to a guest on the phone that the party is only for Audley, since 'the other thing's too big' (p.138). This suggests that Madge and Audley do not quite share the same point of view. As in 'Closer', women's versions of the 'truth' of things are different from men's.

Children have yet another perspective on things. Ned, for instance, 'would if it could be done with honour, have gone out and waved a flag', since he wants 'time to have precise turning-points that could be marked and remembered' (p.152). Ned represents nationalism in its most nascent and apparently innocent aspects. However, his vision of 'a bonfire on every beach and the whole map of Australia outlined with fire' (p.153) carries a hint of danger in its evocation of more extreme and potentially violent forms of nationalism. This is a rare instance of the child's point of view having negative connotations, in comparison to the more passive, less jingoist stance of his elders.

The weight of evidence in 'Great Day', and in Malouf's writing generally, is *against* time having 'precise turning-points'. Although the story contains and generates a certain amount of expectation, its chief incident is the burning down of the local museum. This incident only confirms for Audley, whose point of view the narrative adopts at this point, the impossibility of marking time, since life (at least from this perspective) is merely 'the dervish dance of what is in the last resort dust' (p.177).

Narrative point of view: fluid and shifting

The narrative point of view of 'Great Day' tends to align itself with Audley, who at times becomes a mouthpiece for the expression of a particular world-view (as in the above instance). However, the narrative ultimately avoids settling on any single person's point of view due to its continual play of voices and consciousness.

Thus, the Tylers' party is described not by a single, omniscient narrator but by a narrative voice that shifts from person to person, following the characters' idiosyncratic movements around the rooms and among the guests. Section V begins with Jenny as 'the look-out' (p.159), whose call leads to Madge trying to find room for various food items. Once the party is underway the narrative follows Fran's restless 'hovering' around the room, then shifts to Clem who 'watched [Fran] from cover' (p.162), then back to Fran – 'she came to the edge of a group' (p.164), and so on.

Later, Audley searches for Fran, who has gone for a walk with Angie (in order to avoid Audley). Audley had wanted to ask Fran 'about one or two things' but instead he sips from the glass of wine he had brought her. This action, in turn, generates unanswered questions from the reader: why is Audley's sipping wine 'forbidden, of course' (p.170)? A period of heavy drinking in Audley's past is hinted at (as it is also in the earlier reference to his 'established drunkenness' as a jazz pianist, p.157). However, the absence of witnesses – in particular, the absence of Madge – means that a hint is all the narrative provides.

Audley's perspective on the museum fire is given a final twist when he feels Lily Barnes's 'eye upon him', and he imagines her thinking him a 'sorrowful old hypocrite' (p.178). So, although the narrative makes Audley's point of view highly significant, it simultaneously draws the reader's attention to the ways in which this point of view is constructed and located in relation to *other* points of view. Finally, at the close of the story (and of the evening), the narrative leaves Audley and takes up the perspective of Angie, with whom it began, and the close of one day leads in turn to the expectation of 'a new day coming' (p.185).

Q What are the implications of the phrase '[Audley] had given his bones ... into public custody, which was in some ways the most hidden, the most private place of all' (pp.158–9)? Why does Audley imagine himself as a model of 'ancient, outmoded man' (p.159)?

Q Why do you think the group of strangers who camp on the beach is so fascinating, in different ways, to Ned and Fran? Why is Audley so *un*interested?

Q Why do you think Malouf does not describe the strangers' perspectives or points of view on the Tylers?

CHARACTERS & RELATIONSHIPS

Although there are no characters that appear in more than one story, many characters are linked by filling similar roles in relation to their families or in relation to social expectations and conventions.

We consider two main groups of characters, which themselves are often interlinked: children (including the figure of 'the child') and outsiders. Within each group there are subgroups. An especially important distinction to make is that between characters who are children, and adult characters who recover a sense of being childlike. Writers and storytellers form a smaller group of characters also having strong connections with the groups of children and outsiders.

The child

Key quotes

'Next year, when I am ten, and can think for myself and resist the influences, I will go to school like the boys.' ('Closer', p.25)

'Jordan my name is. Jordan McGivern. I am twelve years old. I can show you this country. I been in it long enough.' ('Blacksoil Country', p.116)

'It was a thing he used to say when he was a little lad of nine or so: "Tell me when I was six," he would say, "when I was four, when I was just born." It was an obsession with him. But no detail you gave was ever enough to convince him that he really belonged among them.' ('Great Day', p.145)

'... stepping into the dark little rooms where everything was so cramped and crowded was for Audley like re-entering one of the abandoned spaces of his childhood ... with all its furnishings rearranged.' ('Great Day', p.155)

The figure of the child takes two main forms in *Dream Stuff*. The first is that of characters who *are* children. These include narrators – Amy, who is nine, in 'Closer', and Jordan, twelve, in 'Blacksoil Country' – and protagonists such as Jack in 'At Schindler's', and a number of minor characters. The second form of the child is that of characters who are *adults*, whose recollections of childhood are central to the thematic concerns of *Dream Stuff*.

Children and love

The child characters provide a relatively innocent perspective on the world, in which people and objects are more connected than the adults in their lives seem to believe. An important feature of this perceived connection is the child's feeling or experience of love. Thus, Amy's love for her uncle Charles and her desire for his (re)inclusion is clearly distinct from her grandfather's exclusion of Charles in order to express love for God. Amy puts this distinction in terms of an opposition between love and death; Charles' banishment implies that he is 'as if he was already dead, and death was stronger than love, which surely cannot be' (p.30).

Similarly, Jordan McGivern declares that he 'loved this place we'd come to' ('Blacksoil Country', p.121). This love is expressed in physical terms, whereby Jordan feels in touch with the country, 'sprawled out flat and your kneecaps touching it, feeling its grit' (p.122). As well, the country touches Jordan, sensually and intimately, when he is 'letting a breeze touch me ... on my bare skin like hands' (p.122). In the end, death and love are not opposed, as Amy suggests, but reconciled, as Jordan blends into the land that he loves, 'making it mine' (p.130).

The child as actor

Ned Tyler, Ralph and Angie's son in 'Great Day', is slightly different from the other child characters, in that he wants *more* order and structure than his parents. He would like the 'party of interlopers' (p.148) on the beach to be excluded, and he feels 'proprietorial, but responsible too' (p.149). He demands information about his family from his mother, so that he will 'know how to act' (p.134): his idea of selfhood, then, is a kind of sustained performance, but one in which the boundaries will not be too negotiable or fluid.

On the threshold of being adult: performance and selfhood

One central character for whom acting and identity are closely linked is Sally Prentiss. At nineteen, she is on the threshold of adult life, a status that is reinforced by her name: 'Prentiss' suggests the role of 'apprentice'. Compared to Ned, Sally has a much less clearly defined notion of the self, less sense of personal property or space. Her 'profession' is to form temporary relationships with American servicemen. This occupation is in keeping with her ambition to become an actor, since she effectively *performs* a role for each of these men. However, because of the central role of sex in these relationships, her life comprises more intensely intimate and invasive experiences than acting, experiences that challenge Sally's sense of having her *own* 'self'.

Sally's experiences shift into a much more adult form when she spends a night with Brad Jenkins and his two young children. In this encounter, sex ceases to be a performance in which she must separate her sense of self from her body's activities. With Brad, physical intimacy becomes connection on a more than physical level. The act of sharing – including sharing the bed with Brad's baby daughter – is also a form of healing, which enables Sally to come to terms with a more comfortable, less weighed-down version of her own self.

Re-entry into childhood

One of Malouf's persistent interests, in these stories and throughout his fiction generally, is in adult experience that, at odd, unpredictable moments, recaptures the revelatory intensities and insights of childhood. This state of being is fundamentally paradoxical. On the one hand, it is located in the past, and seems to be absent from the experience of being adult; on the other hand, it is simultaneously able to be recovered at any time or place. Yet this recovery of the child-within-the-adult invariably takes place at the most *un*expected times, and in places that are in between other places: on thresholds, verandahs, beaches, 'under-the-house' (p.33).

The most fully drawn of the adult characters, the author Colin Lattimer in 'Dream Stuff' and the retired public servant Audley Tyler in 'Great Day', are haunted by their pasts. They are fascinated by the possibilities of being, in some way, in touch with those pasts, and by a state of being associated with childhood, the state of being childlike. This state is represented as being more pure and intense than everyday, adult life.

For Colin, it is attained partly through the creative act of writing fiction. The process of remembering the Brisbane of his childhood, and imagining the persistence of mangroves underneath the present-day city of metal and glass, is closely tied to his writing. Colin's description of characters and places is likened to moving figures around in a childhood game: 'he moved one of his characters into place' (p.43).

In 'Great Day', the Waruna Folk and History Museum contains many of the Tyler family's old possessions, and 'stepping into the dark little rooms … was for Audley like re-entering one of the abandoned spaces of his childhood' (p.155). This 're-entry' is partly a recovery of memories and feelings that might otherwise be lost, remote in the past; simultaneously, it anticipates the end of life, when Audley imagines himself as a relic, 'stuffed and sat there' (p.159) in the museum.

'Great Day' gives many of its men childlike attributes, though with varying degrees of complexity and not always with positive associations. Cedric Pohl, for instance, is called 'a good-looking boy' by Fran, to which Angie retorts: 'He isn't a boy… He's thirty-three' (p.171). Audley's son Ralph retains, as an adult, an element of the childlike: he had 'never grown out of the schoolboy stage of being all arms and legs … he liked to fool about, but then, without warning, would go quiet' (p.140). Ralph's brother, Jonathon, is characterised by a cool indifference to those close to him that makes him remote from the childlike – but which also, in some ways, marks him as the most child*ish* member of the family.

Audley's son Clem has experienced the most permanent and radical form of 're-entry' into childhood, as a result of serious head injuries sustained in a car accident. He asks Madge for details about his past, large sections of which are now 'a blank' (p.145). In the process of recovering this experience, he also takes on the attributes and attitudes of a child. He looks 'very intent, an alert seven-year-old' (p.147); then he rushes to greet Audley, hurling himself through the wire-screen door ... he flung his arms around his father' (p.148).

Clem's intensity and passion make him a far more affectionately drawn character than his more worldly and sophisticated brothers. The narrative takes little interest in what Jonathon or Ralph have to say, but Clem makes some crucial contributions to 'Great Day', in terms of the perspective he makes possible on his family and the questions he asks of them.

Childhood and loss

Clem's most extended and significant moment is his speech towards the end of the evening, one that rings true not only in the context of 'Great Day' but in the context of *Dream Stuff* as a whole:

> If we imagined ourselves out there and concentrated hard enough ... we could hear it too, all of it, the whole sound coming towards us, all of it ... Nothing ever gets *lost*. (pp.180–1)

This draws attention to the role that the experience of loss plays in life, in a way that is ultimately positive and reassuring. This is especially so, given the resonances of the speech with Clem's own recent life experiences, and what he has lost in terms of adult understanding, memory, and relationships. If *Clem* can say this, the narrative implies, *anyone* can believe it and take heart from it.

Key point

The focus on loss also links the narrative back to the experience of Jack in the very first story, 'At Schindler's' – remembering that Clem's speech is placed on one of the final pages of *Dream Stuff*. Clem's words – 'nothing ever gets *lost*' – are anticipated in the description of the Scarborough camping ground, which is a 'city of tents' (p.8) over the Christmas and Easter holidays, and empty at other times. Rather than regretting their lack of permanence, Jack enjoys the coming and going of families and friends; their reappearance, after each interval, is a sign to Jack that 'nothing was lost' (p.9).

By the end of 'At Schindler's', Jack has had to come to terms with his own experience of loss through his realisation that his father will not be returning from the war. This leaves 'a shadow on his heart ... a feeling of loss from which he would only slowly be released' (p.24). This 'feeling of loss' is both negative – represented as a form of captivity from which Jack requires 'release' – and positive – in its liberating qualities, that paradoxically leave Jack 'refreshed, restored' (p.24).

Similarly, at the close of 'Great Day', Clem's speech leaves Audley 'deeply moved' yet also reassured about the loss of the museum, and perhaps also by Clem's capacity, against the odds, to experience 'happiness' (p.184).

Outsiders

Key quotes

'Grandpa has cast him out, as you cut off a limb so that the body can go on living.' ('Closer', p.28)

'It was a strange homecoming. He knew no one in Brisbane but his cousin Corrie.' ('Dream Stuff', p.38)

'She had always been an outsider here ...' ('Great Day', p.166)

Most of the central characters in these stories are, in one way or another, outsiders. Their feelings of alienation and difference may be due to an inability to completely identify with existing social groups, or their perceptions of themselves as out of place. The experience or feeling of strangeness is a key symptom of being an outsider. Colin Lattimer returns to a place he had been very familiar with in childhood but which now seems strange. Jordan McGivern feels love, from 'the minute I first laid eyes on it', for the 'blacksoil country' (p.121), in which the Aboriginal people regard Jordan's family as 'the most strangers of all' (p.127). So, whether a person is an outsider or not depends on whose point of view is being considered.

Outsiders in minor roles

Some minor characters are also outsiders, and it is this status that causes their lives to impact so strongly on the central characters. Uncle Charles is an outsider in 'Closer', exiled from his own family because of his sexuality; the reader sees him from the point of view of a child, Amy. She sees herself as included within the family, but the reader can see that Amy is also partly outsider with respect to the family's adult values of conformity and their willingness to remain within safe, circumscribed boundaries of behaviour. Amy's desire to participate in a larger world than is contained within the secure fences of the family's dairy farm and the strict teachings of their religion, is clearly signalled by her ambition to become an astronaut – an ambition, in other words, to escape earthly limits and restraints.

In 'Night Training', Dave Kitchener is 'a bit of an outsider with his fellow officers' (p.66). The young cadets quickly realise that Kitchener 'couldn't be trusted to keep to the rules' (p.66), but his night drills and lectures do lead to Greg Newsome becoming adept at imagining himself outside the routine, disciplined actions of his body. Perhaps imagining oneself well outside of the main, physical action is the best possible survival strategy once one is an insider within the theatre of war.

Outsiders on the move

In 'Sally's Story', Brad Jenkins is an outsider because his wife has left him. Sally's mother describes him as living 'out Dugan way with two little kiddies' (p.84). Brad's house signifies the precarious, provisional nature of the lives of outsiders, in between movement and stasis: a 'house on wheels, a portable barrack-block ... like a stranded railway carriage' (p.88). Sally is an outsider too, visiting 'home' but soon realising 'why she had left' (p.81).

Being an outsider is often related to being mobile and unsettled. Harry and May Picton in 'Lone Pine' are outsiders in the sense that they leave behind their regular routines of their work and home life. They take a driving holiday and join the 'whole tribes that for one reason or another had never settled ... were always on the move' (p.103). Although for many characters being an outsider enables new insights and possibilities in life, for Harry and May the transformation in their lives precipitated by their being out of place turns out, by sheer bad luck, to be fatal.

The autonomy of the outsider

In 'Great Day' perhaps every character could be regarded an outsider; at least they all seem to see themselves in that light. Madge is an outsider with respect to the establishment, as represented by Audley and the professional circles they have moved in for so many years. Unlike Audley, in whose family 'everything could be traced back', Madge knows nothing about her parents or their backgrounds: in Audley's words, she 'belonged to no one but herself' (p.135). This allows Madge to possess the kind of individuality and independence that is characteristic of outsiders. Curiously, Madge is the one character who never goes outside in the story; instead, she sends the children to gather wild spinach while she remains inside, at the centre of the family's party arrangements.

Writers and storytellers

Characters who are writers or storytellers in *Dream Stuff* are invariably outsiders in some sense. Moreover, their link to their own childhood, or to children, is significant in some way. The novelist Colin Lattimer, for example, has two recurring dreams of childhood that frame 'Dream Stuff'. Colin's first novel had sought to recapture the 'warm sunlight of his Brisbane childhood' (p.44), but it had been written in London, from a remote, 'outsider's' perspective.

In 'Great Day', Fran suddenly feels as if she is 'a little girl again at the lonely fence-rails', a feeling that prompts her recognition that she 'had always been an outsider here' (p.166). Her outsider status stimulates a great deal of writing, as a means of resisting the Tyler family's conventions and expectations. Unlike Colin's writing, Fran's writing remains in the genre of the private confession, in notebooks written 'behind locked doors', and finally 'flushed ... down the loo in a hotel in Singapore' (p.167).

This raises an interesting question about how gender affects writing – whether men and women write differently and for different purposes – and how it affects the way the literary world perceives a piece of writing. Of course, Madge, another outsider with respect to the Tyler family (who is also more 'inside' it than Fran will ever be), is also a writer – of children's books. Unlike Fran, though, Madge publishes regularly, thus achieving a degree of public recognition and success.

THEMES, IDEAS & VALUES

Dreams

Key quotes

'I knew it was a dream. But dreams can be messages. The feeling that comes with them is real, and if you hold on to it you can make the rest real.' ('Closer', p.32)

'... the dreamlike ritual of ordering and presenting arms ...' ('Night Training', p.70)

'They brought it to bed with them, in dreams from which they woke shouting ...' ('Sally's Story', p.78)

'They faced one another like sleepers whose dreams had crossed ...' ('Lone Pine, p.106)

The dreams of *Dream Stuff* are experiences that take individuals out of ordinary life, and enable an alternative reality to be conceived or imagined. The stable categories and divisions that define and structure everyday experience are, in dreams, more readily dissolved or overcome.

In this sense, dreams are like fantasy: they are merely wishful thinking or longing for a more desirable state of affairs, but unable to exert any force on reality. However, the distinction between dreams and reality is frequently blurred in *Dream Stuff,* suggesting that dreams participate in reality as much as they offer a fantasy about it.

Dreams: out of time, out of place

Dreams represent an escape from the boundaries of time and place. When Colin dreams in the police cell, he enters 'a place where there were no walls' (p.55); in his dream at the end of the story he is 'nowhere that can be found on any map' (p.62).

The significance of the term 'dream stuff' for marijuana relates less to the drug's consciousness-altering properties than to its rumoured night-time harvests. According to this story, city teenagers are blindfolded and driven to 'the foothills of the Range' (p.42) – taken out of known places and regular patterns of waking and sleeping. This is akin to the creative process as it is represented through Colin. He is unaware of the passing of time as he writes, immersing himself in the lives and places of his characters; despite Brisbane's tropical heat, Colin feels that 'the room he was writing in seemed within reach of invisible snow peaks' (p.41).

Amy dreams that her Uncle Charles walks through the fence bordering the family property, which represents her desire for this spatial boundary to be crossed. At the end of 'Night Training', Greg Newsome dreams about Cam and imagines 'looking down at the sleeping figure from a height, a distance of years' (p.73); in this case, dreaming is a form of travelling across time.

Dreamlike experiences

The most traumatic events in the characters' lives are described as dreamlike, or they are given an air of unreality very close to the experience of being in a dream. For instance, Dave Kitchener's night-time drills in 'Night Training' seem, to Greg Newsome, a 'dreamlike ritual' (p.70). In fact, on the first occasion Greg thinks Kitchener's intrusion 'must be a dream' (p.67), until its improbable reality is brought home to him by the cold night air.

Other examples of extraordinary, intense experiences are also given dreamlike qualities. Jack's walk along the Schindlers' verandah in the midst of a violent storm occurs immediately after he wakes from a dream, and it retains dreamlike qualities and feelings: being out of control, feeling overwhelmed by sensations, encountering familiar people in unfamiliar attitudes and activities. In Jack's case, these feelings are related to his sense of being returned to a very young age, seeing his mother and Milt's love-making and the double dislocation of identifying his father's ghostly image in the room and then recognising it as his own.

In 'Lone Pine', Harry Picton finds that driving is 'dreamlike ... miles of empty country fell away ... Clouds filled the windscreen. You floated' (p.101). The idea of floating conveys a sense of otherworldliness, a dreamlike escape from physical restraints and ordinary realities. May, in the passenger seat, falls asleep: 'with the lolly in her jaw, its cherry colour seeping through into her dreams' (p.102).

Recognition and misrecognition

When Harry goes to his caravan door in the middle of the night he feels the doorknob turn 'with the uncanniness of a dream-happening' (p.106). The word 'uncanniness' expresses the apprehension of something familiar and homely, which simultaneously seems absolutely unfamiliar and unsettling. The dreamlike nature of Harry and Kenny's encounter is reinforced by their being likened to 'sleepers whose dreams had crossed' (p.106).

Jack's misrecognition of his own image in his mother's mirror is another example of the uncanny, in what is also a very dreamlike experience. Another misrecognition occurs in 'Dream Stuff', when Colin's assailant mistakes him for someone else. Once again, Colin's feeling of being unable to alter the flow of events gives them a dreamlike quality; it is as if 'some agency had taken over whose imagination ... he could neither anticipate nor control' (p.49).

When Jordan McGivern watches his father shoot an Aboriginal man, the narrative of 'Blacksoil Country' invests the incident with dreamlike qualities implicitly rather than explicitly. To Jordan, the Aboriginal people seem 'to bounce on their heels and rise up a little. To float' (p.125). The link between floating and a dreamlike experience is made explicit at the opening of 'Lone Pine' (p.101), and events unfold before Jordan's eyes as if he is in a dream, too.

Later, at the moment of the shooting, Jordan perceives his father as simultaneously both familiar and strange, which gives the incident its uncanny quality. The father 'had a brightness to him I had never seen before ... like he had just hit on a new way of being inside his own skin' (pp.125–6). That is, the father is transformed – and we now consider bodily transformations in more detail.

Experiences of intimacy and transformation

Key quotes

'What Jack was reminded of was moments when, in a kind of freedom only his body had access to, he ceased for a time to be a boy and became a porpoise ...' ('At Schindler's', pp.20–1)

'I will stretch out my hand and touch him, just under the left breast, and he will be whole.' ('Closer', p.32)

'The youth stood. He was a swarming column. His feet had taken root in the earth.' ('Lone Pine', p.115)

'And me all that while lying quiet in the heart of the country, slowly sinking into the ancientness of it, making it mine, grain by grain blending my white grains with its many black ones.' ('Blacksoil Country', p.130)

There are two closely related experiences common in the dreams or intense experiences in *Dream Stuff* – a heightened level of human intimacy and personal transformation.

Transforming feelings

The most obvious example of a dreamt intimacy overcoming a separation is Amy's dream about Charles in 'Closer', in which Charles walks through the fence to the waiting family. In Amy's more conscious imagining, she touches Charles 'just under the left breast' (p.32). Amy's imagination exerts a force on her reality, since it elicits feelings (recalling those of the dream) that she wants to hold on to.

These transformed feelings relate to Amy's desire for a future reconciliation with Charles that will manifest itself in his own bodily transformation: 'he will be whole. He will feel it happening to him' (p.32). What Amy's future actions will be, of course, remains a matter for the reader's imagination, but the transformation of feeling is clearly a valuable first step in any process of reconciliation.

Lightness and weight

Amy's transformed feelings are represented in terms of lightness: 'I had such a feeling of lightness and happiness it was as if my bones had been changed into clouds' (p.32). A similar lightness in Jack's state of mind is evident on the morning following his revelatory moment in 'At Schindler's', when he climbs the hibiscus to a point 'higher than he had ever been before' (p.22). In 'Sally's Story', Brad Jenkins is characterised by his 'capacity ... for being light-spirited' (p.89). In the context of this narrative – after Sally has decided that marriages are best summed up by the word 'woe ... the weight in that word of all that was human and hopeless' (p.81) – Brad's lightness of being signals that he is somehow right for Sally, at least at this time.

The opposite sense is registered in Kenny after he shoots Harry and May Picton in 'Lone Pine'. He too is transformed, attaining a state of tremendous weight: 'his feet had taken root in the earth ... He felt too heavy to move' (p.115). Thus, heaviness is aligned with violence and destruction, and lightness with regeneration, happiness and love.

Interestingly, though, when Jordan's father shoots an Aboriginal man, Jordan perceives that it is 'the moment in his life ... when he felt lightest, most sure of himself, most free' (p.125). This sense of lightness and freedom, quite different from what Kenny experiences in 'Lone Pine', partly explains, in psychological terms, the father's actions and the 'monstrous' bearing he acquires following Jordan's death. His capacity to draw other men to him, to inspire the killing of many more Aboriginal people, is couched in terms of their being '*lifted out* of the ordinary business of clearing scrub' (p.129, our italics).

Physical intimacy and emotional distance

In 'Night Training', Dave Kitchener forces Greg Newsome to undress the sleepy Cam Brierly. This is more intimacy than Greg desires, and it causes him and Cam to move apart emotionally. Thus, physical intimacy – the proximity, in this case, of two naked male bodies – does not necessarily lead to emotional closeness, and invariably it is the latter that Malouf is most interested in.

Similarly, Sally Prentiss is physically intimate with a number of American soldiers, but these experiences are denied much of their potential emotional force by Sally's ability to 'touch without touching' (p.79). In contrast, Sally's spur-of-the-moment encounter with Brad Jenkins brings both physical intimacy and an emotional closeness, which is paradoxically enhanced by the presence in bed between them of Brad's baby daughter.

Transforming into the land

In various ways, *Dream Stuff* gestures towards a form of belonging to place that transcends age, race and nationality. In this respect, one interesting transformation is the merging of bodies and the earth.

This transformation has its most metaphysical form in 'Blacksoil Country'. The deceased narrator, Jordan, describes the process of his body's parts merging with the soil. The soil is 'black' in a double sense: its colour, and its property of belonging to Aboriginal people – pointing to the invasive nature of white settlement. However, Jordan's white body is 'slowly sinking into the ancientness of it, making it mine, grain by grain blending my white grains with its many black ones' (p.130).

This process suggests a fusing of land and identity, whereby white settlers (and their descendants) can acquire a form of indigeneity in Australia akin to that of Aboriginal people. As Jordan says, 'I can show you this land. I been in it long enough' (p.116). Non-Aboriginal Australian attachments to place are considered in more detail later, under the heading 'Settlement'.

Spaces underneath, on the edge and in between

Key quotes

'Barefoot ... he stepped outside and, like a child younger than his present self, a six-year-old still scared of the dark, started off down the verandah to where his parents slept.' ('At Schindler's', p.20)

'The slats that closed in their under-the-house made the place dim, even in daylight.' ('Dream Stuff', p.33)

'It was a secret place down here. With the sea on one side and the cliffs on the other, you were walled in, but ... you didn't feel its narrowness, only a deep privacy.' ('Great Day', p.171)

Dream Stuff's characters frequently have intense, dreamlike experiences in spaces that are in between. In 'At Schindler's', Jack's shock at seeing his father's image, then recognising it as his own reflection, occurs as he stands on the verandah, in front of the open French doors to his mother's room. He is not quite inside, out of the storm, nor is he entirely outside.

Other examples of in-between (or liminal) spaces in *Dream Stuff* are its many boundaries, thresholds and edges: fences, doorways, beaches, and the space under the house. In-between spaces are metaphors for and projections of characters' experiences of personal transformation and revelation. In addition, in-between spaces provide the very conditions necessary for those experiences to take place.

Key point

In *Dream Stuff*, a person's external world, and their internal, psychic world, are not separate, but interactive and mutually determining. Identity is produced as much by the environment (including the material, constructed environment) as by that which is inherent in a person.

In-between spaces are contested sites, where the question of who holds the most power is not completely decided. This contest may be relatively gentle, as when Colin Lattimer, as a child, remains under the house despite his father's appeals for him to return to the household. Or the contest may be a matter of life and death, as in 'Blacksoil Country', when the policing of boundaries that are recognised differently by Indigenous and non-Indigenous characters results in a series of murders.

Under the house

The space under the house figures at the beginning and ending of 'Dream Stuff'. It belongs to the house, but its 'forest of stumps' and 'the big dog warm in [Colin's] arms' (p.34) suggest a more primitive, sensual landscape. The tension between natural and socially constructed worlds characterises Colin's remembrance, at least in its dreamt form, of this childhood episode. It also structures Colin's adult perception of Brisbane, with the city's 'flyovers, multi-level carparks, tower blocks' (p.36) underlaid by a more natural, primitive landscape of 'roots in mud' and 'the stick-eyes of crabs and their ponderous claws' (p.42).

A similar tension exists in 'Jacko's Reach', reflecting on the forms of behaviour possible in a wild, undeveloped space but prohibited in conventional social spaces. The proposed shopping mall, skateboard ramp, tennis courts and Heritage Walk all gesture towards a social life that is well ordered and in plain view. This is the double meaning of the opening phrase, 'so it is settled' (p.93): it is 'settled' that Jacko's reach is to be developed, and the process of development will also attempt to settle down the abnormal life that Jacko's Reach has hosted for so long.

The beach

Beaches are typical in-between spaces. They are between land and sea, and they are constantly transforming. The flux of a beach's existence offers a good analogy to the ebb and flow of feeling in dreams. Thus, at Schindler's, the 'sound of the sea would find its way into [Jack's] sleep' (p.1). In a later dream, Jack is at the top of the slippery-slide on the Scarborough beach 'with a king tide running' (p.19) shortly before his own life undergoes something of a tidal change.

Beach and dream are also linked in an intriguing scene in 'Great Day'. Angie and Fran walk down to the water to escape from Audley's party and find themselves in a 'secret place', 'the sea on one side and the cliffs on the other, you were walled in' (p.171). They are outside, in a public space, but simultaneously they experience a 'deep privacy', as if within the walls of a room.

As Fran and Angie walk around the beach they come across the strangers, but their state of privacy persists and they 'plump down in the cool sand to spy' (p.172). Fran imagines herself walking over to the fire among the strangers, lying down to sleep then dreaming. However, Fran's vision of herself as at peace among a group of strangers is not reflected in her later solitary behaviour, when she leaves the party alone and 'closed her mind to everything but the drive ahead' (p.181).

Thresholds

Doorways, passageways and gates are thresholds: they are conduits between spaces as well as border zones. The open tent flaps of the Scarborough holiday-makers' tents signal ease of access and the feeling of having 'nothing to hide' ('At Schindler's', p.8). On the other hand, the many gates through which the Tylers' guests must pass in 'Great Day' signify privilege and exclusivity.

The caravan door in 'Lone Pine' becomes the threshold of a catastrophic event. In his ordinary home, Harry would presumably guard the front door strictly – as suggested by the care with which he installs a home security system. However, the caravan is a mobile rather than a fixed home, and the Pictons adopt an informal approach to their holiday routines. Harry's momentary lapse in vigilance allows Kenny to enter unchallenged, and costs the Pictons their lives.

Fences

Fences play an important role in *Dream Stuff,* both literally and metaphorically. In 'Closer', the fence symbolises social segregations and exclusions, which lead to loss and unhappiness. The separations represented by the fence are reinforced by words that prohibit rather than communicate. Charles approaches the fence, before his father warns:

'Don't come any closer' (p.28). In response, Charles 'walks up and down outside the fence and shouts' (pp.29–30). In Amy's dream there are no words spoken, and when Charles reaches the fence he walks 'right through it' (p.31).

In 'Lone Pine', fences are associated with Harry and May's safe, comfortable lives in suburban Hawthorn: 'Harry tossed the news over people's fences on to the clipped front lawns' (p.102). The end of Harry's life, however, is represented in terms of a space in which 'the distances were enormous and there was no fence in any direction' (p.115). It is as if Harry and May have been 'fenced off' from each other for too long, and the distance between them becomes 'enormous' once they cross the final boundary, from life into death.

The property in 'Blacksoil Country' is 'a run of a thousand acres, unfenced and not marked out save on a map' (p.116). On the colonial frontier, the act of fencing transforms a wild space into a settled one. What Jordan refers to as 'our rightful boundaries' (p.122) are not marked on the land itself, nor are they recognised by the Aboriginal people, who know, in turn, a complex set of territories entirely invisible to the white settlers. Malouf thus draws attention to the ways in which fences and property boundaries generally are cultural constructions that ultimately depend on violence for their power to be enforced.

Settlement

Key quotes

'... if, in tribute to settled convention, you did say "knock, knock", it was a kind of joke ...' ('At Schindler's', p.8)

'Being settled was important to him ...' ('Dream Stuff', pp.45–6)

'So it is settled.' ('Jacko's Reach', p.93)

'When we come it was to settle.' ('Blacksoil Country', p.116)

'There is ancient and irreconcilable argument in us between settlement and the spirit of the nomad ...' ('Great Day', p.177)

Since boundaries in *Dream Stuff* are so fluid, these stories raise the question of who legitimately owns or possesses space, and how properly settled it can be. The issue of settlement runs through all the stories, sometimes merely through the notions of 'being settled', or of 'settled convention'. Moreover, settlement often invokes its opposite, unsettlement, as Audley's thoughts on an 'ancient and irreconcilable argument in us' suggest (p.177).

The issue of settlement intersects with understandings of indigeneity, with Australia's colonial history (post-British settlement) and with representations of Aboriginal people. This is especially so in the two final stories, 'Blacksoil Country' and 'Great Day'.

Aboriginal identities

Aboriginal people make several appearances in these stories, always brief yet highly significant. In 'Dream Stuff', the lock-up's atmosphere of barely restrained violence is enhanced when 'three or four black youths were being dragged to the door of his cell, shouting obscenities' (p.55). The 'blacks' help invest the cells, at least for Colin, with their utter strangeness, and make the signs of state-sanctioned violence and oppression far more tangible.

Elsewhere, Aboriginal people are more the subjects of historical episodes than present-day realities. Jacko's Reach was formerly known as Jago's but, for the narrator, its current name is a 'black one' and thus signifies, albeit belatedly, the land's 'original owners' (p.94). In 'Blacksoil Country', Jordan's narrative is an imagined colonial child's perspective on Aboriginal people. At first the blacks seem strange and vaguely simple: they 'dance and shout', then 'squealed and run about' at the firing of a gun (p.123). Later, Jordan reverses the perspective, so that Aboriginal groups are seen to have a complex understanding of territory, while the McGiverns appear 'the most strangers of all' (p.127).

Space invaders and the 'superior sense of belonging'

'Great Day' invokes national issues and histories in an oblique manner, focusing instead on personal and familial affiliations. However, the issues of indigeneity, invasion, and reconciliation are all implicit in Ned's innocent-seeming observations of a group of strangers on the nearby beach. This moment stages a reversal of the colonial encounter, in which white colonisers arrive on a beach with the intention of dispossessing the black Indigenous inhabitants of their land.

Ned is threatened by the arrival of visitors, one of whom is dressed, as Ned sees it, as a 'space invader'. Correspondingly, Ned smears his face with dark ashes and pretends to be 'a spirit of the place' (p.149). In contrast, the visitors' complete lack of real attachment to this place, as Ned sees it, is summed up by his opinion that: 'these others were tourists' (p.149).

The scene is ironic, because from the point of view of Aboriginal people, Ned and his family might also be considered to be 'space invaders', 'tourists' who have stayed for too long. Ned's 'superior sense of belonging' is made possible largely by the absence of Aboriginal people watching on and drawing Ned's attention to his own strangeness on this shoreline. However, the narrative denies Ned's position any real credibility, since his performance of indigeneity, with his face covered in ashes and his presence so easily discovered by the 'space invader', is rather comic.

For Ned's child's imagination, the roles of native and invader are slippery: either one can be performed by all parties. However, the Tylers' ownership of this land seems so natural to Ned not because anyone can legitimately identify as a native of any place in the world, but because of the patrilineal nature of property inheritance (meaning that it is passed on to male descendants). Ned simply imagines no reason to question the handing down of property: 'this headland and the next as well belonged to Audley and would one day be Ralph's, then his' (p.149).

Settlement and unsettlement in 'Great Day'

In one way, Audley Tyler's family represents white Australia at its most settled and comfortable. Audley is descended 'from two colonial worthies' (p.135) and his house is a 'four-square structure of sandstone blocks, very massive and permanent looking' (p.132). Audley's name is similar to the word 'orderly', and his life does follow an orderly pattern in some ways: he always wears a 'black suit and tie' (p.132), he regularly takes a walk in the afternoons and he plays the piano last thing at night. In other respects, though, the course of Audley's life has followed no set pattern; in this respect too it is like the house, to which rooms have been 'added on in the style of the times' (p.132).

Ned objects to his family's almost random or improvised way of living: 'they like things left up in the air. They never want anything settled' (p.152). The narrative also resists settling things, and leaves a number of questions unresolved – in particular, what kind of relationship now exists, and has existed in the past, between Audley and the Aboriginal man Tommy Malloy?

'One of the unsettled'

The title of 'Great Day' itself points towards unsettlement. It derives from an Inuit poem, which is recalled by Audley as he watches the local museum burn down. The poem describes 'the great day that dawns, the light that fills the world', though it is not entirely clear what is being referred to here. Audley does not think of this poem as written specifically by the Inuit people of far North America (for whom it could mean the first dawn following their winter of near-constant darkness), but merely as by 'one of the unsettled' (p.177).

In what Audley thinks of as an 'ancient and irreconcilable argument in us between settlement and the spirit of the nomad' (p.177), his sympathies lie with the nomadic (at least at this moment). This is rather disingenuous, since Audley is clearly one of the nation's more privileged citizens. His whole life has been devoted to the patterns of settlement – to having a family, a large house, a well-paid job, and a position of power within the community and the nation.

Non-Aboriginal belonging: seeking to legitimate settlement

Ned's attachment to the Tylers' land is expressed as a 'superior sense of belonging here, of knowing every rock and stump on this hillside as if they were parts of his own body' (p.149). This 'sense of belonging' is entirely personal, a feeling that relates the land to Ned's own body. A similar, non-Aboriginal, bodily connection with the land is represented in 'Blacksoil Country', in which Jordan's body blends with the soil, becoming part of it – belonging to it, in other words.

In *Dream Stuff* generally, the issues of settlement, indigeneity and belonging relate more to people's feelings than to legal and political definitions of land and property ownership. The ideology suggested here poses difficulties in the context of the contemporary politics of Aboriginal identity, land claims and reconciliation in the twenty-first century. That is, if belonging to the land is mostly a question of feelings, then non-Aboriginal people can claim to 'belong' to a place on much the same basis as Aboriginal people.

Thus, feelings of belonging to the land work to legitimate the ways in which land, in turn, belongs to white Australians. If 'settler' and 'native' are more or less interchangeable categories that can be blended and merged (as in 'Blacksoil Country') or performed by any person with a lively imagination (such as Ned in 'Great Day'), then it would seem that reconciliation is an already accomplished fact.

Seeing things 'out of another history'

By contrast, as Audley meditates on the burning down of the museum, he sees that his Aboriginal friend, Tommy Malloy, is 'standing a little way off to the left … and as always seeing the thing, the fire in this case, out of another history' (p.178). The difficulty with expressions of non-Aboriginal belonging is that they merge Aboriginal ways of seeing into non-Aboriginal ways of seeing. This merging of radically different perspectives and histories is logically problematic and politically contentious, since Aboriginal and non-Aboriginal Australian claims to place are made from radically different positions of power.

This, perhaps, signals a limit or boundary beyond which dreams cannot reach. Beyond this limit, those 'other histories' need, for ethical and political reasons, to be told as much as possible by Aboriginal peoples themselves. In a way, Audley's silent recognition of Tommy's radically different way of seeing things can be interpreted as a tacit acknowledgement of a liminal zone. In this in-between zone, the power of dreams begins to fade. If any further understanding is to be gained, the dream world, the in-between world, has to be left behind so that real dialogue and negotiation can begin.

QUESTIONS & ANSWERS

This section focuses on your own analytical writing on the text, and gives you strategies for producing high-quality responses in your coursework and exam essays.

In writing on a collection of short stories, your response will depend crucially on which story or few stories you focus on. Try to balance detailed reference to two or three stories with your display of knowledge of the collection as a whole. Don't discuss the stories individually as if they are completely isolated from each other, but move confidently between stories, showing connections between them as well as variations and points of difference.

Essay writing – an overview

An essay on a literary work is a formal and serious piece of writing that presents your point of view on the text, usually in response to a given topic. Your 'point of view' in an essay is your interpretation of the meaning of the text's language, structure, characters, situations and events, supported by detailed analysis of textual evidence.

Analyse – don't summarise

In your essays it is important to avoid simply summarising what happens in a text.

- A **summary** is a description or paraphrase (retelling in different words) of the characters and events. For example: 'Macbeth has a horrifying vision of a dagger dripping with blood before he goes to murder King Duncan.'
- An **analysis** is an explanation of the real meaning or significance that lies 'beneath' the text's words (and images, for a film). For example: 'Macbeth's vision of a bloody dagger shows how deeply uneasy he is about the violent act he is contemplating, and conveys his sense that supernatural forces are impelling him to act.'

A limited amount of summary is sometimes necessary to let your reader know which part of the text you wish to discuss. However, always keep this to a minimum and follow it immediately with your analysis of what this part of the text is really telling us.

Plan your essay

Carefully plan your essay so that you have a clear idea of what you are going to say. The plan ensures that your ideas flow logically, that your argument remains consistent and that you stay on the topic. An essay plan should be a list of **brief dot points** covering no more than half a page.

- Include your central argument or main contention – a concise statement of your overall response to the topic.
- Write three or four dot points for each paragraph, indicating the main idea and evidence/examples from the text. Note that in your essay you will need to *expand* on these points and *analyse* the evidence.

Structure your essay

An essay is a complete, self-contained piece of writing. It has a clear beginning (the introduction), middle (several body paragraphs) and end (the last paragraph or conclusion). It must also have a central argument that runs throughout, linking each paragraph to form a coherent whole. See examples of introductions and conclusions in the 'Analysing a sample topic' and 'Sample answer' sections.

The introduction establishes your overall response to the topic. It includes your main contention and outlines the main evidence you will refer to in the course of the essay. Write your introduction *after* you have done a plan and *before* you write the rest of the essay.

The body paragraphs argue your case – they present evidence from the text and explain how this evidence supports your argument. Each body paragraph needs:

- a strong **topic sentence** (usually the first sentence) that states the main point being made in the paragraph
- **evidence** from the text, including some brief quotations

- **analysis** of the textual evidence, with **explanation** of its significance and how it supports your argument
- **links back to the topic** in one or more statements, usually towards the end of the paragraph.

Connect the body paragraphs so that your discussion flows smoothly. Use some linking words and phrases such as 'similarly' and 'on the other hand', though don't start every paragraph like this. Another strategy is to use a significant word from the last sentence of one paragraph in the first sentence of the next.

Use key terms from the topic – or synonyms for them – throughout, so the relevance of your discussion to the topic is always clear.

The conclusion ties everything together and finishes the essay. It includes strong statements that emphasise your central argument and provide a clear response to the topic.

Avoid simply restating the points made earlier in the essay – this will end on a very flat note and imply that you have run out of ideas and vocabulary. The conclusion should be a logical extension of what you have written, not just a repetition or summary of it. Writing an effective conclusion can be a challenge. Try using these tips:

- Start by linking back to the final sentence of the second-last paragraph – this helps your writing to flow, rather than leaping back to your main contention straight away.
- Use synonyms and expressions with equivalent meanings to vary your vocabulary. This allows you to reinforce your line of argument without being repetitive.
- When planning your essay, think of one or two broad statements or observations about the text's wider meaning. These should be related to the topic and your overall argument. Keep them for the conclusion, since they will give you something 'new' to say but still follow logically from your discussion. The introduction will be focused on the topic, but the conclusion can present a wider view of the text.

Essay topics

1. "Not a ghost, but himself, fantastically elongated in the glass of the old-fashioned wardrobe."
   'In *Dream Stuff*, the shock of misrecognition forces characters into a new state of heightened self-awareness and maturity.' Discuss.

2. "They feel a kind of shyness in the presence of the father."
   Discuss the roles of fathers in *Dream Stuff*.

3. "There was a strangeness. Some of it was in the light. But some of it, he knew, was in him."
   To what extent do the changes in the lives of characters in *Dream Stuff* depend on their experience of 'strangeness' in a previously familiar world?

4. "Nothing is lost. Nothing ever gets *lost*."
   Discuss the role of loss in *Dream Stuff*.

5. "I had to look at it in a whole new way."
   'The insights and understandings gained by the characters in *Dream Stuff* come not so much from new experiences but from new ways of looking at known things.' Do you agree?

6. "She had always been an outsider here …"
   '*Dream Stuff* shows how it is often the people on the outside of conventional social groups who have the truest perceptions of reality.' Discuss.

7. How does *Dream Stuff* show the importance of a sense of belonging?

8. '*Dream Stuff* suggests that dreams can transform realities.' Do you agree?

9. "A whole lot of different things happened to that boy. If they'd happened to Ralph he'd be just like it."
   To what extent do the stories in *Dream Stuff* suggest that identity is determined by external events and influences?

10 '*Dream Stuff* explores the diverse consequences for human beings when the rules and conventions of daily life are suspended or revealed to be arbitrary.' Discuss.

11 "There is ancient and irreconcilable argument in us between settlement and the spirit of the nomad ..."
Discuss the ways in which this 'argument' is played out in *Dream Stuff*.

12 "Things had been moving towards some event or revelation that at the last moment, for whatever reason, had been withheld."
Discuss the significance of the withholding of revelation for selected characters in *Dream Stuff*.

13 "So it will be gone and it won't be. Like everything else. Under."
What meanings are symbolised in *Dream Stuff* by spaces that are 'underneath'?

Analysing a sample topic

"She had always been an outsider here ..."

'*Dream Stuff* shows how it is often the people on the outside of conventional social groups who have the truest perceptions of reality.' Discuss.

First, consider the topic's contention: do you agree? The key terms are: 'outside', 'conventional social groups', 'truest perceptions' and (perhaps) 'reality'.

What makes a character an outsider? How does this enable them to see the world truthfully?

You might take 'truest perceptions' to be those least affected by social conventions. A problem is that truth in *Dream Stuff* largely depends on whose point of view is being considered; therefore there is a question about whether there is any objective 'reality' to be perceived. However, the stories generally prefer certain points of view – such as those of narrators – to others, and it would be hard to sustain an argument that truth is completely subjective in *Dream Stuff*. Moreover, social conventions are represented as essentially arbitrary, able to produce misleading appearances and distort the truth.

The context of the quote

Think about the context of the quote, 'she had always been an outsider here'. This is Fran's feeling about herself in relation to the Tyler family in 'Great Day': she sees Angie's daughter, Jen, and remembers being 'a little girl again at the lonely fence-rails' (p.166). This links being an outsider with childhood and with borders or edges (the fence-rails in this instance).

In what ways are Fran's perceptions of the Tyler family more truthful than those of its other members?

Examples of outsiders

Which other characters are 'outsiders'? Consider Colin in 'Dream Stuff', Clem in 'Great Day', Uncle Charles in 'Closer'. You could include the child characters, such as Ned in 'Great Day', Amy in 'Closer', Jack in 'At Schindler's'. Children might be *outside* the adult world of power, money, sexual relations and so on, but *inside* the family group – dealing with this complexity could make your answer more interesting.

Focus on just a few characters, whose outsider qualities are varied. Which social group or groups are they 'outside' of?

The insides and outsides of groups are not clear-cut

The association between perceiving truth and being on the outside is not completely straightforward. Some individuals on the inside of social groupings also seem to apprehend the truth of things, even though the narrative tends not to adopt their point of view.

In 'Great Day', Fran watches a group that includes her former boyfriend, Jonathon. Her point of view highlights the artificiality of those about to laugh at a judge's joke that they already know (p.164). Fran seems accurately to perceive people's social posturings here – but then, so does Jonathon: he is inside the group but he winks at Fran, indicating that to some extent he shares her 'outsider' point of view.

Amy's child's understanding of her Uncle Charles' banishment in 'Closer' seems more natural or 'true' than the rigid rules of the Pentecostal church by which the family lives. However, the perspective of the character who is really on the outside of this family – Charles – is not available: would his point of view be any more or less true than Amy's?

Conclusion

In conclusion, draw together your analyses of the various outsiders in *Dream Stuff*. Give a clear, concise response to the topic and refer explicitly to its key terms. If you agree that outsiders *do* have the truest perceptions of things, what does this imply about conventional social groups and their effects on individuals?

SAMPLE ANSWER

Discuss Malouf's exploration in *Dream Stuff* of the ways in which people respond to loss.

Boys who lose fathers, parents who lose children, husbands who lose wives, individuals who lose their past – all these are aspects of loss explored in *Dream Stuff*. The ways in which characters respond and develop reveal their inner complexities, vulnerabilities and strengths.

Jack's father, in 'At Schindler's', was the third point of a triangle, 'somewhere over the horizon', a triangle of which Jack and his mother were the other two points. Jack's father was 'missing in action' in World War II, where 'missing' is like 'walking into a cloud'. At first he is invoked at every meal, at changes of the season; Jack emulates the way his father dives into the pool at Schindler's, and works hard to conjure up the tone of his father's voice. However, Jack's mother gradually moves on, facing the increasing certainty that her husband will not return. The changes in her, reflected in the mirror which she shares with her sister as they prepare to go out, and her growing relationship with the American serviceman Milt, make Jack uneasy. He feels more and more that his own faith in his father's return is the 'slender thread' that keeps his father alive.

His faith is finally shattered when, after waking from a nightmare in which he is stranded on the slippery-slide, he sees his mother in bed making love with Milt. At first Jack thinks it is his father returned; then it is as if his disillusionment has raised the ghost of his father, standing forlornly by the bed – but in fact it is his own reflection in the bedside mirror. This device is used by Malouf to represent Jack's identification with his father (and we are told Jack is growing to resemble him), his allegiance to him which is now being put to the test, and the need for Jack to confront and respond to this change in his life. He does manage, after some soul-searching, to accept that his father will never return, and to move on positively, albeit 'with a shadow on his heart', into a new phase of his life.

Malouf again uses the image of a son almost seeing the ghost of his dead father in 'Dream Stuff'. Colin retraces his dead father's steps as a tourist in Athens – at any moment he expects to see his father walk around the corner. Instead, Colin is deserted by his erstwhile guide, lost in a labyrinth of streets. Colin has also lost – in some sense – his past life. He returns to Brisbane as a successful author and contacts his cousin Corrie, with whom he shared an intimate and exclusive relationship as a child. He seeks this old intimacy, their old language, but fails to find it. It's there, but not there, in the same way as he seeks the old city he knew, which he intuitively knows is just beneath the veneer of the new city, glimpsed in the same quality of light he knew as a boy. The loss of his first marriage is a further instance of the features of his life that have slipped away or been overlaid by other lives.

Clem, in 'Great Day', has lost his past in a more total sense. Through this character, Malouf explores how an individual responds when put into the position of having to reconstruct his life and his identity. Clem's head injury in a car accident has erased his memory. He must start again, relying on his family and his ex-wife to fill in vast gaps, to tell him stories about himself as a child and reassure him of their love for him. Yet it is also Clem who, perhaps having learned through this process, reassures his father Audley, after a fire that has destroyed all the family memorabilia, that 'nothing is lost. Nothing ever gets *lost*.'

This notion that 'nothing is lost' is also explored in 'Blacksoil Country', in which a twelve-year-old boy loses his life and a father loses his son. Father and son have a complex relationship. Jordan possesses skills and qualities that the father lacks; he is aware of his father's shortcomings, but is unquestioningly loyal to his father. When Jordan becomes a victim of the consequences of his father's prejudice and racism, murdered by Aboriginal people in revenge for the murder of one of their own, Pa is distraught. However, Pa's new status as a grieving parent gives him an altered identity, and an enhanced rapport with other white settlers. Thus, Pa's loss of Jordan leads to a discovery of another self, which at last gives him some pride.

Moreover, there is a deeper sense in which Jordan is not lost. He remains tied to the land, to the Blacksoil Country. Malouf describes this in almost mystical terms as Jordan sinking into the soil, becoming part of its fabric: 'blending my white grains with its many black ones'. This is true in a physical sense; it is also true in a historical and metaphysical sense. Jordan's death precipitates a violent response that permanently changes the course of history in this area, and the course of relations between Aboriginal inhabitants and white settlers. Jordan becomes an almost mythical figure, the lost child, yet in his own telling what endures is his own attachment to the land and the possibility he represents of a more harmonious form of settler belonging to place.

There is a further paradoxical sense of deep loss inextricably linked with gain in 'Sally's Story'. Sally participates in the construction of a myth for American servicemen on leave from the Vietnam War. She performs the role of wife for men acting out a domestic fantasy; significantly, the term used for her job is 'widow'. At the end of their leave, the parting is a wrench for the soldiers returning to battle. This loss is not of the substance of happiness, but only of its shadow. Their farewells and embrace of loss are translated into physical action as they gee themselves up to go: 'Huh huh huh, on ten now!' In contrast, Brad's loss is one he faces with quiet, loving fortitude. While still a boyish, boisterous man, he is steadfast in caring for his two children, covering the loss of their mother with a reassuring mantra: 'We got ourselves, eh?' The concealed pain of this loss is revealed to Sally when she opens the cupboard in Brad's bedroom to find all his wife's clothes still hanging there.

In 'Dream Stuff' Colin faces a series of losses, which to some extent he masks by incorporating his memories into his fiction. The story opens with the imminent loss of the family dog, Maxie, dying of heartworm beneath the house. This is Colin's earliest memory, forever linked to the image of his father gasping with hayfever, reaching out to retrieve his son. Their fingers do not meet; just as Colin seems never to have made a deep connection with his father, who later drowned during the war. At different times of his life Colin has created islands of happiness that have now disappeared – his childhood relationship with his cousin Corrie, his first marriage and closeness with his infant children, his feeling of oneness with the Brisbane of his youth. Yet these losses are not absolute; Colin's memories are part of the fabric of his life, waiting just beneath the veneer. So too is his current relationship with Emma in London, who wakes to his phone call and reassures him that this other life is not lost in the nightmare of Colin's arrest.

Malouf explores many aspects of loss, while constructing images of things persisting even if past – just as Jacko's Reach, with all its stories and history and myths, will persist under the tarmac and mushroom lights of the new carpark. Although these losses are profound and have lasting effects, they can also lead to growth and be accompanied by the possibilities of new sources of happiness.

REFERENCES & READING

Text

Malouf, D 2001, *Dream Stuff,* Vintage, Sydney.

Further reading and viewing

Autobiography

Malouf, D 1985, *12 Edmondstone Street,* Chatto & Windus, London.

Newspaper and journal reviews

Craven, P 2000, 'Shock of recognition', *The Sydney Morning Herald,* 1 April, Spectrum, p.10.

Hassan, I 2000, 'In dreams begin reconciliations', *Australian Book Review,* 219, pp.39–40.

Lorenzo, O 2000, 'The rhythms of life', *The Age,* 18 March, Saturday Extra, p.7.

Other references

Elizabeth W 1984, *Psychoanalytic Criticism: Theory in Practice,* Methuen, London & New York.

Reynolds, H 1981, *The Other Side of the Frontier,* UNSW Press, Sydney.

Videos

Featherstone, D (dir.) 1997, *An Imaginary Life: David Malouf – Author,* Sydney, Film Australia.

Tipping, R (dir.) 1987, *David Malouf: An Imaginary Life,* Sydney, Artwrite pictures.

Websites

Daniel, H 1996, 'Interview with David Malouf', *Australian Humanities Review*, Issue 3, September, http://australianhumanitiesreview.org/1996/09/01/interview-with-david-malouf/

Jones, T 2015, 'Interview: author David Malouf speaks to Tony Jones', https://www.abc.net.au/lateline/interview–author–david–malouf–speaks–to–tony–jones/6366484

Koval, R 2014, 'Transcript: David Malouf in conversation with Ramona Koval', *The Monthly*, https://www.themonthly.com.au/book-club/2014/april/transcript